T0290377

PENGUIN BUSINESS

EQUAL, YET DIFFERENT

Anita Bhogle, a postgraduate in statistics (IIT Mumbai) and also in management (IIM Ahmedabad), has reinvented herself almost every decade. Her early years were spent in advertising, market research and marketing consultancy. For the next two decades, she, along with her sports broadcaster husband, Harsha, ran a highly successful motivational series called 'The Winning Way—Learnings from Sport for Managers'. The series translated into a book of the same name, which sold over 1,25,000 copies and started a new genre in motivational speaking. Anita went on to set up Bizpunditz, India's first video-learning library for managers, which was eventually sold to an edtech company. A mother of two sons, Anita is a yoga and sudoku enthusiast, and an amateur keyboard player.

PRAISE FOR THE BOOK

'Anita, in writing this book, has gifted us all a true guide and created a new manifesto for an equal world'—Shradha Sharma, founder and CEO, YourStory Media

'*Equal, Yet Different* is full of ideas on what career women need to do to become the best versions of themselves . . . she mentions not only areas such as networking and managing finances but gives equal importance to health, nutrition and exercise'—Rujuta Diwekar, nutritionist and author

'A book both men and women must read to bring true diversity to the home and workplace'—Rashmi Bansal, bestselling author

'A simple yet thought-provoking read that I recommend not only to all those who aspire to make a mark but also to those who support them in fulfilling their dream'—Rachana Ranade, entrepreneur and finance content creator

'A book that does not speak in generalities and actually maps out an action plan for women in the workforce. I plan to implement a lot of her excellent advice and you should too'—Naomi Datta, author and television producer

EQUAL,
yet DIFFERENT

Career Catalysts for
the Professional Woman

ANITA BHOGLE

BUSINESS

An imprint of Penguin Random House

PENGUIN BUSINESS

USA | Canada | UK | Ireland | Australia
New Zealand | India | South Africa | China

Penguin Business is part of the Penguin Random House group of companies
whose addresses can be found at global.penguinrandomhouse.com

Published by Penguin Random House India Pvt. Ltd
4th Floor, Capital Tower 1, MG Road,
Gurugram 122 002, Haryana, India

First published in Penguin Business by Penguin Random House India 2022

Copyright © Anita Bhogle 2022

ISBN 9780143459279

Typeset in Adobe Garamond Pro by MAP Systems, Bengaluru, India

www.penguin.co.in

For my parents, Lily and Ramakant Kulkarni,
my role models for hard work and integrity

My husband, Harsha,
whose phenomenal success has strangely been both a hurdle and
an enabler for my career

My sons, Chinmay and Satchit,
good students but better teachers to me

Keru, Mangesh, Anusaya and other members of the staff, who
made my journey comfortable at different times in life

Contents

Introduction

In December 2013, I unexpectedly found myself seated next to the amazing Narayana Murthy, who was in a very relaxed and jovial mood. My husband Harsha and I had been invited as guest speakers by Infosys to its Mysuru campus. We had just finished our presentation to their senior leadership team, and since there was still some time for lunch, they had organized for us a tour of the impressive campus. To our utter joy, Mr Murthy decided to accompany us in the buggy, so there we were, discussing sport, business and other fun things. I remember there was a bench in the middle of a sprawling lawn and he insisted we have a picture taken on the 'love seat'! Busy young men and women were making their way across the enormous campus on foot or on bicycles. We were told that the well-lit campus had state-of-the-art lighting, making it safer for the large number of young women who worked and lived there. The air smelt of freedom and opportunity. As we finished the guided tour, I said to Mr Murthy, 'I am jealous.

I wish I was born twenty years later.' He smiled and took it as a compliment to their commitment to diversity, and then we chatted a bit about building a culture of meritocracy and equal opportunities.

The last two decades have seen a healthy number of women graduate from a wide variety of professional courses in all fields, particularly from management institutes, engineering colleges, law schools, medical colleges and architecture schools. Many make it to the honours list or win medals, and a significant number go on to study further and earn a master's degree or even a doctorate. A visit to any office complex will convince you that men and women have nearly equal representation there. There is no doubt at all that women have it in them to excel in all of these careers. Unlike sport, professions like management, chartered accountancy, medicine, law, architecture and most engineering streams have an advantage as they don't involve any physical prowess, making gender differences irrelevant to careers.

Yet, when you look at the lists of prominent and successful alumni of the very same colleges or office-bearers of industry forums in any of these fields, you will find very few women there. According to Deloitte Global's Women in the Boardroom report—2022, a global average of just 19.7 per cent of board seats are held by women. In India, it is a shade less at 17.1 per cent, and even among this, only 3.6 per cent of the board's chairs are women. Compared to the 4.5 per cent figure in 2018, it has dropped by 0.9 per cent over the years. It is an effort to find strong women candidates for leadership and board positions in companies. Even those who were front runners at the start of the race have only a small chance at a podium finish. To what extent does gender become a liability or prove to be a hurdle in the path to success?

For far too long, the term 'glass ceiling' has been bandied about as an explanation for this phenomenon, but I feel it is a rather simplistic and somewhat dubious way to explain the entire situation. It is not like the old days when women were not allowed entry into all-male clubs. Men are not conspiring to hold women back. But bias, whether it is conscious or unconscious, still exists around women's capability and ambition. There are many more missing pieces in this puzzle, not all of which have to do with our work and careers.

Today, women are trying to straddle two equally important but very different worlds. For professionals, work life is very demanding, high pressure and competitive. Those who aspire to remain on top of their game need to give time, energy and focus to their work. At the same time, as nurturers, we remain the ideal caregivers when it comes to our families. Look around and you will find that urban, working women, whether single or married, are increasingly taking on the responsibility of looking after their parents and even siblings. Bearing children is a biological reality, while caring for the ailing and the aged is a social one, especially in the Indian context. Unfortunately, we don't have an adequate and well-managed infrastructure for either childcare or eldercare. Furthermore, many sections of society frown upon such arrangements, forcing women to take on that role full-time and putting an end to their career aspirations. What can the family do to help a woman pursue her dreams? How can organizations ensure that, after becoming mothers, women don't get permanently sidelined? A well-managed home is, without doubt, the stepping stone to a successful career. Knowing that the needs of the family are being attended to sets the mind free to focus on one's career. Do spouses merely say that they are proud of their wives' achievements or are they truly supportive in sharing the physical and mental load of bringing up a family and managing a home? The lack of support at home forces a very large percentage of women to recalibrate their ambition. The demand for equality at the workplace has been loud and forceful, but women and their aspirations need equal consideration in the home as well.

For a long time, women assumed that the only route to equality was to try and be like men. We have come full circle, to a time now when gender differences are being celebrated and organizations realize that teams benefit from diversity. Years of conditioning in a patriarchal system have ensured that women are wired differently from men. Women are taught to think about others first; so you could be the most celebrated CEO but when you come home, you become a selfless homemaker. Guilt remains the exclusive preserve of women and is omnipresent!

Women view success very differently from men. Most of them don't openly chase designations or flaunt success symbols for the outside world to see. A woman's identity does not come from her career alone. She is a professional, a wife, a mother and more, rolled into one. She views success as the ability to balance these roles in the best possible manner. It was amazing to see the variety of ways in which this balance is being achieved by the women I spoke with and how each one's idea of equilibrium is different from someone else's. Unfortunately, some of this conditioning and related behaviour comes in the way of career success and needs to be unlearnt. Diversity has the potential to strengthen teams; it should not become its weakness.

The challenges that women face are well known and well-documented. I wanted to find out what those who have managed to stay on track have done right. When we look at women achievers in India, there are the usual trailblazers who are often quoted, but there are a number of other women too, who have managed to make their mark despite not being that visible. You will find some of their stories here. I also wanted to know how women who have had to either compromise on their careers or give them up completely feel about their situation. Was it the most sensible decision? Do they have any regrets? Looking back, could they have done things differently? Indian, or perhaps Asian women are different from their western counterparts in that family plays a much bigger role in our lives, and our parents and spouses have a substantial say in the choices we make. That is a significant factor, since even the personal life choices that we make impact our chances at professional success.

Early in my career, I spent a number of years doing qualitative market research, conducting group discussions for various product categories. Not only did it give me tremendous insights into how consumers think, but as a bonus, I gained some personal skills as well. Till then, I had been quite a nerd; quiet, serious-minded and introverted. Constantly interacting with groups of strangers and encouraging them to share their experiences transformed me as a person. In due course, I became far more social, outgoing and capable of drawing out the most unlikely people!

Even today, I remain a researcher at heart, so when it came to writing this book, I did not want to limit it to my experiences alone. Through my personal and professional network, I sought out women professionals with different profiles—single, without children, with children. I included women from different communities, across all age groups and working in different sectors. The idea that others should benefit from their experience appealed to everyone I spoke with, and they were generous with their time and their insights. They bared their hearts as they shared the most personal stories about how their bosses, their parents or their spouses impacted their career choices. They were candid about their own insecurities and their joys as well as their successes or failures as they navigated their careers. Some of the stories were more like emotional outpourings, so in order to protect the privacy of the storyteller and those who feature in the story, I have masked their identities. In all, there were around ninety women who I interviewed in detail, either personally or via email. There were CEOs, HR heads, researchers and teachers as well, who shared their observations and provided an organizational point of view. So, this book is not mine alone. It is a crowdsourced effort that has dipped into the wealth of experience of so many!

Every day you read about the path-breaking achievements of women in all fields. Teachers, nurses, journalists, and increasingly, pilots, bureaucrats and so many others are making valuable contributions to society. While I believe that this book would be of interest to all career women, there is a reason I have deliberately focused my research on women with professional qualifications. In competing and through qualifying in challenging exams, they have displayed both their ability and desire to have careers at the highest level. They have spent time, money and energy to pursue their dreams and have much to lose, should they have to give it all up. They are the ones who will lead the way and give a voice to the rest of the women. Their success will have a trickle-down effect into smaller towns and lower socio-economic classifications (SECs), for those who are grappling with more significant glass ceilings. They will be shining beacons and visible role models for future generations.

This book is for young professional women who will learn about where the potholes lie, what they need to watch out for. As a generation, millennials are the first to enjoy the advantage of having a fairly large pool of professionally qualified women that they could learn from. If they can gain from the experience and wisdom of the generations before them, my effort would be well-rewarded.

It will help the men in their lives to understand women and what makes them equal, yet different. It will also be useful to all those who are invested in them—parents, spouses, bosses, HR professionals. They constitute the ecosystem and are potential enablers to a woman's career. Their involvement and attitude can either help her succeed or become hurdles to her progress.

While the challenges seem universal, the answers are not standard. So, while reading the book, it may be interesting to look at what worked or didn't work for others, but remember that you need to explore your own solutions. This can only be achieved through reflection, introspection and an understanding of your own dreams as well as your circumstances. To help you do that, I have put down some points at the end of each chapter. I hope you will take time to pause and think, rather than merely speed-read the book, looking for answers.

I hope the stories of determination I have written in the book will inspire some of you and give you the courage and strength to pursue your goals. Many mantras have been shared, and I am sure that they will leave you with ideas on how to navigate your life and career. Above all, I hope the spirit of sisterhood with which so many women have shared their failings along with their achievements will give you the hope that those who have the courage to dream are also blessed with the strength to realize those dreams.

We live in a time of great opportunity, and it would be foolish to waste it. Unfortunately, it is also a world where opportunity is not as fairly and evenly distributed as ability. If we, as a society and a country, are to achieve maximum potential, it will be both a pity and a waste if this precious national resource pool of talented and qualified women does not have equal access to this opportunity. After all, as Mao Zedong said, 'Women hold up half the sky.'

Chapter 1

Equal, Yet Different

I have spent much of the last twenty years building content for 'The Winning Way'. It is a motivational series in which my husband Harsha and I speak about management lessons from sport. Sometime in the early 2000s, we were doing a session for senior executives from the Tata group. In those days, it was not very common to see women in top management and, at most, there must have been two or three women in the audience. During the interaction that followed the presentation, I met Sangeeta Talwar, who I subsequently discovered was the first woman FMCG executive in India. She told me that she loved the presentation but there was one slide that particularly resonated with her. It had a quote from Steve Waugh, former captain of the Australian cricket team.

'As a leader, you need to treat your teammates equally, yet differently,' he had said.

'That is so applicable to women,' said Sangeeta. 'That is exactly how women want to be treated.'

Equally, yet differently! Steve Waugh had said that in the context of how leaders need to build teams. First there are the non-negotiables like integrity and team ethic where the rules are the same for everyone; everyone is treated equally irrespective of performance or experience. And then there are the little exceptions, the small liberties, the slightly different treatment that you allow your key players. If the star players are in the right frame of mind, it helps them give their best and the team's performance improves. Accommodating without compromising!

Women are a significant part of most teams today, and while they might need some flexibility from time to time, their performance needs to be weighed on the same scale as everyone else. The Steve Waugh quote is a powerful statement for diversity and inclusion, and was made way before the issue even started getting discussed in corporate circles. Equal, yet different stayed with me for many years and came back to me as I thought of writing this book.

Sport is all about inspiration, emotion and passion. During our sessions, we tell a lot of stories about sportspeople and champion teams. Our presentation, too, is visually powerful with each picture telling a story. When we started 'The Winning Way' two decades ago, all our slides had male athletes. I don't know if it is a coincidence that as Indian girls started winning and we began to proudly add photos of Sania Mirza, Saina Nehwal, Mary Kom and then P.V. Sindhu, Dipa Karmakar and others, we found, much to our delight, that the number of women in the audience had also steadily increased.

'The Winning Way', as I mentioned, is about learning from sport for managers. As the name suggests, the book and our presentations address the issue of winning and success. Our belief has been that if you have a decent level of skill or ability and combine it with great attitude and work ethic, you are likely to do well in whatever you do, whether it is sport or business or music or medicine. The real masters, the ones who make it to the top of their profession, have an extra ingredient over and above ability and attitude. They are consumed by passion or obsession with their art or trade. We call this the winning triangle—ability, attitude and passion being its three angles. Over the years, we have talked about this idea, and most people seem to accept this concept of the winning triangle.

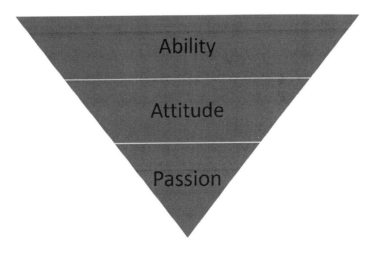

Over the last ten to fifteen years, I have found that the young women in the audience appear far more confident and articulate. They seem less inhibited while discussing their ambitions and their challenges. In the early days too, there were things they wanted to talk about or they had questions on some of the topics discussed, but they preferred to do it in private, after the session was over. Along with the new-found confidence, I have also sensed in them a certain restlessness or reservation with the idea of the winning triangle, as if they were not entirely convinced that this was enough to ensure success. After some more probing and soul-searching, it became apparent that there is a fourth side, a fourth angle that affected women far more than men.

The personal choices that a woman makes—marriage, the choice of spouse, whether she chooses to have children, how many and at what age—not only go into determining her career path and how successful she might become but also play a significant part in shaping her personality. Choices affect men as well, but for women, they have far greater implications. Even now, it is the women who are expected (and are willing) to relocate after marriage, change gears once the kids arrive and make adjustments when the family requires caregivers. The same amount of ability and attitude doesn't always take women the same distance as it would take a man, because very often they are denied the luxury of being passionate about their work without worrying about anything else.

If you ask a man to describe himself, he will probably say that he is a doctor or an engineer or an IT guy. His identity is, more often than not, completely defined by his profession. A woman sees herself as a wife or a mother along with being a career woman. Her identity is fragmented and therefore rooted in the choices she makes.

Clearly, the triangle isn't enough. For women, there is a significant angle that is beyond the triangle—it is the choices they make.

Women, Ambition and Careers

Dr Saundarya Rajesh and her company Avtar have done pioneering work in the area of career intentionality. Career intentionality is a term used to describe a woman's commitment to her career, its place and importance in her life, and her determination to continue with it in the face of the many challenges that she faces at various stages of her life. It addresses issues such as whether women take charge of their careers, have specific goals and work towards achieving them. Your career intentionality score indicates whether you drive your career in a specific direction or allow it to just happen.

Statistics show that nearly half of the Indian women professionals abort careers midway, before they even reach the mid-career mark.[1] This is 19 per cent more than the Asian average. Of the 48 per cent of women who take breaks in their careers in corporate India, nearly 18 per cent (annually) do not return to the corporate world, practically disappearing from the work radar. Interestingly, this percentage is not attributed to maternity alone.

Based on Avtar's 2015 study on career intentionality of Indian professionals, it was found that gaining professional expertise was the key aspiration for both men and women in the early career stage (less than five years of experience). By the mid-career stage, career achievement became the significant priority for men, while it was work–life integration for women. At advanced career stages, both men and women sought work–life integration. Would it be right, then, to say that ambition is not constant but depends upon your priority at a particular stage in your life and therefore on the choices that you make?

As we go through life, either alone or along the way adding a husband, children and ageing parents to our list of responsibilities, some of us manage to walk the tightrope, others settle for more manageable options, while many just swallow their personal ambition and abort their careers. Every point on the spectrum is crowded with thousands of women with their own unique stories to narrate. I have made an attempt to take snapshots of as many points as possible.

While a great deal of ambition depends on a woman's personality, the seeds are sown in childhood itself. It can be a challenge for those who come from traditional communities or conservative households with no working women in the family for reference. A woman's societal role models are the women in her family, and if they have run their homes a certain way, then that becomes the norm for her. Before you know it, society's expectations start becoming your own expectations of yourself. Breaking out of that mindset requires a lot of grit and perseverance.

Family dynamics impact a woman's career far more than one would imagine. An older brother in the family gets parents involved in his education and career, and younger sisters can piggyback on this involvement. Families with only daughters often focus on their marriage rather than higher education. An older husband already has a head start in terms of salary. The scales already tip in his favour, and there is little chance that the younger wife can demand that her career be given equal priority. One or two maternity breaks could mean that the woman falls further behind in terms of negotiating power. When in a crunch, pure economics takes over, and the career with the lower income automatically gets sacrificed.

Predictably, professional role models play a critical role in increasing career intentionality among women. Not having enough women as senior counsel in the Mumbai and Delhi High Courts gives younger lawyers the feeling that it must be a difficult dream. Most architects visible in the public space are men, and hardly any prominent architectural firms are headed by women, which makes one wonder where all the bright girl students from architecture colleges disappear! Companies with women in leadership roles are looked upon as employers of choice by women professionals, not necessarily at the campus recruitment stage but certainly as they approach middle management and start thinking seriously about work-life balance. On the home front, having mothers, aunts and sisters who are working means that the younger ones don't quit their jobs unless there is no other option.

Till recently, Shivani worked for a digital marketing and communications agency. Recently married, she would work even over weekends, and while she made it home before dinner, she would need to log in right after. That is the norm for most young professionals in India, but it makes life difficult for those who have responsibilities at home.

'In my agency, as with most advertising agencies, most of my colleagues were young, the women didn't have kids and there was a culture of working late,' she observed as she explained her struggle with her schedule. With no time to connect with friends or even with her own self, Shivani has now moved to an organization that works for a cause she strongly believes in and also appears to have a less demanding schedule.

Those who grow up with middle-class values of financial independence automatically have a higher chance of staying on course, and even if the family is financially secure, they take their careers seriously. Equated monthly instalments (EMIs) on home loans and other such financial commitments shared jointly with spouses leave the woman with no option but to continue working, even when faced with hardship. She can also expect more support and cooperation from the family as her financial contribution will be valued.

Social conditioning in the early years has a significant impact on the extent of a girl's desire for a career. Did your parents say that home and family are a woman's primary responsibility? Or was it that you needed to be educated enough to be able to stand on your own feet? Did they make you believe that you deserved the best of everything and could grow up to become whatever you wanted to be?

As I researched for this book, I spoke at length with several women in the age group of twenty-eight to sixty-five years. The verdict seemed almost unanimous: today's parents are supportive of their daughters' careers. Unlike the previous generations, where parents got their girls educated with the sole objective of finding a highly qualified groom, today's parents would like to see their daughters have careers and become financially independent. To that extent, the needle has moved but not enough to convert that support into ambition. So, while they encourage their daughters to appear for qualifying exams to get into professional courses, they don't necessarily egg them on to try for the top-ranked institutes or the best-rated courses.

When you look around, you will notice a similar pattern when it comes to women. While there are enough lady doctors, there are very few surgeons, lots of MBAs in HR but few in investment banking, more lawyers choosing the corporate route but lesser numbers in litigation. It is ambition that is laced with caution, softer options that would ensure better work-life balance, where family gets a much higher priority over career!

Professions like management, medicine, law, chartered accountancy, architecture and even engineering, as I have suggested before, have the advantage that there is no strength or physical prowess involved, making gender differences irrelevant. Management institutes, engineering and medical colleges and architecture schools have healthy numbers of women, not only at the entry level but also on their merit lists. Most office set-ups now have women accounting for nearly 50 per cent of their employee bases. There is no doubt at all that women have it in them to excel in all of these careers. Yet women are almost invisible when it comes to decision-making roles or positions of power and influence.

In India, competitive exams to get into professional courses are very tough. The fact that you have qualified proves your ability and capacity for hard work beyond doubt. The growing number of women in all such courses could only point to a starting line that looks far more robust than before. Equality should not even be a topic of debate any more. However, sometimes, being different is perceived as being weak or unequal. That mindset needs to be corrected by undoing the social conditioning of several decades.

Are women differently wired from men, and if so, how does that impact their careers?

Generally, women have an external locus of control and frequently look for validation for their actions or decisions. They can get very bothered by small mistakes. Even someone like writer, speaker and management consultant Rama Bijapurkar, who is such a confident woman and who always seems sure of what she says, confessed that after every talk she gives, her family jokingly asks about 'the 5 per cent'. Rama tends to worry about the 5 per cent of the audience that may not have warmed up to the talk instead of the 95 per cent that probably loved it. We need other people to tell us how well we performed; our own assessment of our achievements tends to be less glowing.

Matthew Mott was coach of the Australian women's cricket team that won the T20 World Cup in 2020. Matthew had only worked with men's teams before he got this assignment.

'The one thing I have noticed,' he says, 'is that, if you're talking to a room full of female athletes and you say something you think is quite a generic statement, every female in the room will think you're talking directly to her. If you do the same thing in a male dressing room, the players will nod and agree—and think the coach is talking about the idiot beside him!'

They may have been trained to be top athletes, but as women, the conditioning appears to be uniform the world over!

Corporate life is no different, according to Rishi Gour, who has led large teams at multinational firms. 'Over the years, one big realization has been that men and women respond to feedback very differently. I think women take feedback very personally and, as a leader, you need to be conscious of this.'

Women tend to be perfectionists and hold themselves to high standards. This can be very tough in workplaces that tend to be uncaring or ruthless. My advice to young women leaders, therefore, is that if there is one thing you need to possess over and above the attributes that male leaders require, it is a thick skin, and the sooner you develop it, the less likely you are to suffer. We women are too hard on ourselves and focus far too much on the brickbats, while not being comfortable accepting the bouquets. We take things far too personally and don't pat ourselves on the back often enough. I find myself guilty of this ever so often. Harsha and I have a unique format for our talks wherein we share the stage and speak as a pair. It has become a ritual now that after the presentation is done and we are back in our room, we rate our own performance. 90 per cent of the time he rates our performance higher than I do. I tend to fuss over small things that we had planned to talk about but forgot, only to be reminded that no one else besides us would have known, least of all the audience.

Many of the women I spoke with admitted that at some stage or the other, they have been hesitant to step out of their comfort zone and try something different, even when the organization is willing to offer them the opportunity. Funnily, while we battle the chauvinistic voices outside that constantly question if the female gender can handle challenges, there is an even bigger struggle raging within us, an inner voice that constantly cautions us against biting off more than we can chew. Often, courage and a thick skin can help tackle the chauvinists, but it takes more than that to silence self-doubt. At some level, these might sound like sweeping generalizations. While it is true that women in their twenties are very different from those in their fifties, some of these traits are too deep-rooted and have become part of our conditioning. Enough women exhibit similar behaviour for it to become a gender stereotype.

Falguni Nayar has led teams at both Kotak Investment Bank as well as Nykaa. She says she has seen too many women fearful of taking up leadership responsibilities, afraid that their work-life balance will go for a toss. After all, leadership does demand a lot of time, energy, focus and commitment.

'Constraints and glass ceilings are only in your mind. To get to leadership positions, women need to ensure that their life is about them as individuals and what they want. They can't just be part of a family structure,' says Falguni.

A widely quoted report based on a study[2] by Hewlett Packard revealed that, when offered a job, men focus on the skills they have while women focus on the ones they lack. It is a proven fact that men display confidence that is far greater than what their ability justifies. Women, on the other hand, show diffidence even when they possess the required ability. This is what Sheryl Sandberg means when she says in her book, *Lean In*, that men put their hand up when they are 70 per cent ready while women hesitate even if they are 120 per cent ready. The impostor syndrome visits women far more often than it does men, the feeling that one is not good enough or qualified enough or simply not quite ready to handle the assignment.

Trishna Shah, an Indian Institute of Management Ahmedabad (IIMA) graduate with fourteen years of work experience, completely agrees with Sheryl Sandberg and says she has observed it first-hand.

'I can say this from experience that so often when my male colleagues have talked about closing a deal in meetings, I have subsequently found out that they are at the exact place in the sales funnel as I am (and I wouldn't think of declaring a deal closed unless it was much closer to actually signing paperwork).'

Anita Sanghi, the only woman senior vice president at NTT DATA Services in India, tells of an interesting encounter with Ginny Rometty, CEO of IBM. Back when Anita was at

IBM, she met Ginny, who was not yet the CEO, at a women's round table. 'As women, we doubt ourselves and I asked her if she had ever felt it,' says Anita. Ginny was very candid and shared that she was indeed very familiar with the feeling but that she had turned that into a positive and prepared better than most men. Others confirmed that it was absolutely true. Ginny, they said, put in a lot of research and hard work and was always well prepared. She had converted her doubts into strengths.

Since men are less prone to suffering from self-doubt and also less inclined to expressing their insecurities to others, they appear more confident as compared to women. Organizations sometimes mistakenly interpret this confidence to mean that the man is better prepared for the role and eager to take on the responsibility. A woman who looks and sounds unsure gets sidelined, and that only reinforces her suspicion that there is some kind of a glass ceiling. So, while unconscious bias does exist, women are equally capable of ruining their own chances!

I must confess that I am not unfamiliar with the impostor syndrome myself. Harsha and I have worked together for almost two decades. While he definitely brings the celebrity quotient to the offering, building it up to be what's probably the most-sought-after speaker series in the country has largely been a result of my efforts. Harsha and I started off as batchmates at IIMA, but about eight or nine years into his career, he morphed into a full-time cricket writer and broadcaster. Standing atop the two strong pillars of cricket and television, he became a household name in India. So much so that when he ran into Lata Mangeshkar in the elevator once, she gave him a smile of familiarity, adding that she felt he visits her living room every day! I have often joked that when I speak alongside him, I feel like the non-striker at the other end when Sachin Tendulkar is batting in full flow. When the spotlight is so completely on him, I need to remind myself from time to time that while he brings the flair and the distinctiveness to the programme, I have brought business acumen and built solid content over the years, which is what made clients come back to us repeatedly. And while he agrees that I can't do what he does, he says he is certain that he wouldn't be able to do what I do either. It helps keep the impostor syndrome at bay—an infrequent visitor, not a regular feature.

Sometimes, small things can help build self-worth. When my earlier book got published in 2011, the publisher suggested that we could have a photo of the two of us prominently on the cover. Our immediate reaction was one of horror. I remember reacting similarly when we first started watching American game shows and saw contestants clapping for themselves! Our middle-class Maharashtrian backgrounds had drilled into us that one should not blow one's own trumpet and this sounded suspiciously similar. The publisher, however, held his ground and insisted that this was the latest trend. This decision was instrumental in introducing people to me and my work. Shyness is an old-fashioned virtue that has lost its relevance in the modern world.

Not speaking up while in a group is yet another behaviour that needs to be unlearnt. Women are very self-conscious and have a fear of sounding stupid or being misunderstood in a meeting. Being a minority, all eyes are on a woman the minute she opens her mouth. It is also possible that men get to know each other better through their informal interactions and so are more relaxed even when they meet formally.

It seems clear that much of what makes us different is the way we are conditioned. But there are other factors as well. For a woman who has responsibilities at both work and home, it can be a tightrope walk because support systems that you create with care have a way of failing when you least expect them to, or worse, when you need them the most. That explains why women, when they make career choices, opt for predictability over the excitement of a challenge. A woman who had all the makings of an equal contender at the starting line then has a very different career graph by the time she gets to the finish line.

A popular life hack for high productivity and success is that you need to give 100 per cent to whatever you are doing. This roughly translates as, 'Don't bring work home and leave your home behind when you come to work.' Women are made to feel guilty if a maid calls during office hours or a parent-teacher association (PTA) meeting comes up on a weekday. The impression created is that women are not focused on work and are easily distracted by things at home. How practical is it to compartmentalize work and home then, particularly for women, when jobs are no longer nine to five?

Nandini Dias, former CEO of the leading media agency Lodestar UM, says that she realized quite early in her career that the work ecosystem—clients and colleagues— 'expects' to have access to employees beyond office hours, but the reverse is a clear red flag. 'So, while dropping a message or a quick call beyond working hours is par for the course, a woman (particularly) is made to feel guilty if, say, there is an urgent call from home or she expresses inability to be available during the weekend. The perception seeded is that women are preoccupied because they come with a handicap called "home". The presumption is that domestic matters can be put on hold but office matters are always urgent. Failing to adhere to these expectations, the individual gets characterized as someone who is easily distracted, not focused, etc., often leading to adverse implications on one's career. Strangely, this same label did not apply to anyone who's busy on social media during a work meeting. It's almost as if a distraction at work is all right as long as it's not "domestic" and it's not happening to the "woman".'

My own feeling is that since the pandemic has forced most people to work from home, the lines between work and home have blurred even further. In such a situation, work-life balance is not as much about making time to finish both office work and domestic duties but about seamlessly integrating both into one's daily routine.

Working late hours has become a norm in the country, especially over the last decade, and it is only now that companies are becoming aware of the risks such a lifestyle brings. In many companies, the unwritten rule is that you cannot leave the office before your boss. So, if the boss is a workaholic with no interests or hobbies, you can say goodbye to work-life balance!

A friend of mine from the Indian Institute of Management Calcutta (IIMC) tells an interesting anecdote about what happened when the company where her husband is the CEO introduced a policy to discourage employees from working late. When, despite the policy, folks continued to work long hours, they realized that the boss himself needed to leave early so that the others would follow suit. 'Leaders leaving loudly' is a practice that is being encouraged all over the world where seniors announce that they are leaving on time so that juniors don't have to pretend to be hanging around or feel guilty about enjoying time with the family.

Anjali Mohanty, senior career banker and now co-founder and CEO of a fintech, remembers with regret that till her daughter was ten years old, she never accompanied her to a single birthday party. In the early stages of her career, she invariably worked long hours. While the bank never expected its employees to work late, it was her own insecurity or perhaps a desire to show her commitment that led her to put in the hours. 'I worked late as a junior and I still work late as a senior,' she laments. She finds that millennials look for greater work-life equilibrium and are better at integrating home and work responsibilities in the day. Now she advises youngsters not to stay back unnecessarily, merely to give the impression that they are hard-working. She does not want them to have the regret that she has.

Despite all the factors that tend to hold women back, when some of us manage to break into the top echelons of our professions, it is certainly a reason to celebrate. The puzzling thing is that while a successful man is loved by one and all, successful women are very unpopular. Is that just the irony of our gender or do women who reach leadership positions have different challenges?

I remember asking a senior woman executive about the working style of a successful woman CEO, one whom she knew personally but I didn't.

'She is an alpha male draped in a saree,' was her description.

In several informal conversations, I have heard men and women speak about their women bosses in similar terms.

One of the reasons is that women leaders have tried to gain acceptance into the leadership circle, which is essentially male, by moulding themselves after the male leaders they have observed. They probably see their gender as a liability and want to break free from negative stereotypes so that they can blend in. Some of it can be mere posturing but they invariably come across as being aggressive and unapproachable. For fear of being seen to be partial to their own gender, they go to the other extreme and are particularly inconsiderate to other women. One of the theories is that, having come up the hard way, making a number of sacrifices on the family and home front, they don't want the younger ones to have it any easier. Strangely and without realizing it, they are actually perpetuating gender discrimination.

In a world where a woman who tries to be assertive gets labelled aggressive, can you imagine what happens to women who try to be aggressive? Powerful men are accepted, maybe even expected to be loud and arrogant, but women are said to make difficult and unpopular leaders.

Rama Bijapurkar has a theory about why women in senior positions are more aggressive than their male counterparts: 'A random sample of male leaders follows the standard normal distribution curve. Women, on the other hand, are few and face so many hurdles that at every hurdle, many fall off the ladder and only the aggressive ones survive and make it to the higher level. By the time you reach the very top, there is a concentration of aggression!' Trust the professor to come up with a statistical model to explain everything!

'Senior women are often accused of having sharp elbows if they are assertive and ambitious. Sometimes women need to be more assertive just to be heard!' says Anjali Mohanty. There are plenty of male leaders who are aggressive, insensitive or plain incompetent, but women being in much smaller numbers attract more scrutiny and more criticism.

The archetypical leader is seen to rule with a firm hand, so anyone who is polite, soft-spoken or considerate is not taken seriously. Women fall into this trap easily and lose their inherent strengths, such as empathy, and the ability to understand people and manage relationships.

Anjali tells an interesting story about a woman boss she had. She was a wonderful American who Anjali respected, grew to be very fond of and was very comfortable with. The woman-to-woman bond was obvious and they often went to dinner or even shopping after work. One evening, over a drink, the boss said she wanted to give Anjali some feedback.

'You are far more hierarchy conscious with men,' she said, implying that Anjali was showing a lot more deference to her male bosses. The lady was demanding more respect, probably suspecting that as a result of the familiarity or friendship, she was being taken for granted! Women leaders often fear that they will be branded as mother hens or agony aunts. Their conditioning tells them that leaders must be respected and distant.

'If you are too empathetic, it gets difficult to get work done,' says Priya, a Mumbai-based intellectual property (IP) lawyer with over eighteen years of work experience.

Over the years, women have struggled with what kind of image is ideal for them as leaders. Is it better to be respected and feared rather than to be liked? A busy image makes you look important but unapproachable, but a friendly image allows others to take you for granted and not respect your time. The ideal mix, of course, would be to be demanding and uncompromising when it comes to performance but show your soft side on the numerous occasions that leaders face when compassion and kindness are required.

Research[3] shows that a key personality trait traditionally held against women while being considered for leadership positions is that women are emotional creatures and lack the ability to stay calm in pressure situations. The fact is that while men and women experience emotions equally, women tend to express them more than men. Expressing emotion is equated to not being in control and, therefore, seen to be a female weakness. Funnily, when as part of the stereotype-shedding behaviour, you find women leaders not expressing emotion, they are labelled cold but still not confident and in control like the men. In recent times, with EQ (emotional quotient) being seen as a desirable trait among leaders, these perceptions will hopefully change. Authentic leaders don't hide their emotions but, more importantly, don't allow emotions to cloud their decision-making.

The image of the male leader is so firmly etched in everyone's mind that for many years, formal dressing meant a black suit, even for women. Jewellery was kept to a bare minimum. The idea was to clone men, not stand out as women. It is very refreshing to see that, in the last few years, colour and jewellery have entered corporate boardrooms.

Among women now in their forties, I am happy to see more who are far more comfortable in their skin. Just as the shadow of the British Raj has finally left India, making us more comfortable and confident about our Indian-ness, women leaders too, are learning to be more confident of their femininity while still focusing on becoming effective leaders. This is very important, since a leader needs to be authentic and comfortable with who she is and not try to be someone else; in this case, certainly not a man. This can only strengthen the case for having diversity in the boardroom.

1) Rate yourself on a 1–10 scale for career intentionality and reflect on how it could be made higher.
   a) Have you identified the next role that you would like to move to? Do you have reason to believe that it will make your CV more attractive?
   b) Where would you like to see yourself at the end of your career? Have you shared your ambition with anyone at home or at work? What challenges do you expect during this journey?
2) We discussed career-limiting attributes such as looking for validation, being a perfectionist, refusing to step out of the comfort zone, focusing on your limitations rather than your strengths, etc. How many of these have you experienced? How could you have done things differently?

3) If you are hoping to go to the next level at work, what are the top two things you will need to work on? How will you go about achieving that?

Chapter 2

Dream Aloud

Falguni Nayar was sitting under a massive tree in the garden of her home in Alibaug while we were chatting over a Zoom call. Falguni, as many of you would know, is the woman behind the beauty business Nykaa. Nykaa is now a listed company whose market cap at the recently concluded initial public offering (IPO) is $7.2 billion. That makes Falguni a billionaire and India's richest self-made woman! To me, Falguni is more than her success story. She and I were batchmates and dorm-mates in IIMA. I am very proud of how well she has done for herself, more so because she has done it all on her own steam.

'I have always been *ziddi*, yaar,' she says, when I ask her to analyse her phenomenal success. That, to me, translates as somewhere between determined and stubborn.

'Knowing what you want and pursuing it. Like even this dream house that we built,' says Falguni, her gorgeous villa serving as the perfect backdrop for the conversation.

The problem is that we need many more Falgunis in leadership positions in order to be heard. When we passed out of IIMA in 1985, we were just nine girls in a batch of 180. That embarrassing statistic of 5 per cent is now up to a healthier figure of 25–30 per cent across various IIMs. Having realized the importance of diversity in classrooms, the admission process has been rejigged to make sure that it is not skewed towards selecting only male engineers. This intervention by the institute has been hugely successful, especially in achieving better gender diversity. We are told that it has resulted in more vibrant class discussions. In a sense, we seem to have found the direction forward, at least at the entry level. However, the problem of fewer women in leadership and board positions persists.

A study[4] by Credit Suisse Research Institute released in October 2019 says that women accounted for just 15.2 per cent of corporate directors in India. The same study shows that India has the third-lowest rank among countries in the Asia-Pacific region when it comes to women CEOs and CFOs, with numbers as low as 2 per cent and 1 per cent. The pattern is identical even in the case of architects, doctors, engineers, chartered accountants and lawyers. There is now a mandate that there must be at least one woman member on the boards of publicly listed firms. But we all know that a directive like this, while being a quick and effective leveller of sorts, is neither desirable in the long run nor does it do anything to strengthen the pipeline.

As Dr Saundarya Rajesh of Avtar puts it, 'The optics are deceptive.' Women continue to drop off the corporate ladder at an amazing rate, and few manage to make it to the top. We start with equal dreams, but somewhere along the way the dreams decouple. Women like Falguni are the encouraging exceptions and, therefore, great case studies for success.

When I look back, Falguni was no different from the rest of us. Simple, hard-working, middle-class. Falguni's story has been one of remarkable achievement in the corporate world. In her first avatar, she rose to head Kotak Investment Bank but it is in her second avatar, as the founder of beauty business Nykaa, that she has truly achieved superstardom. As the head of a multibillion-dollar company, Falguni represents what it is possible to achieve through sheer hard work and enterprise. When I ask her why she threw away a successful corporate career and decided to be an entrepreneur, she puts it down to being an adventurer at heart, a fearless person capable of taking open-ended risks.

In a world where women's career graphs are dotted with safe options, Falguni's story stands out as she has consistently embraced challenges that sounded exciting, without being daunted by the newness of the situation.

In the mid-nineties, when she decided to quit her job at Kotak Mahindra Bank in Mumbai to follow her husband on a transfer to London, Uday Kotak asked her if she would set up a London office for them, when she had absolutely no experience handling legal or compliance issues. Setting up an office for the bank in a new country would involve a lot of that. She took it up, nevertheless. When she started Nykaa in 2012 at the age of fifty, the seasoned banker had a lot to learn about the unfamiliar beauty business. She was merely a first-time entrepreneur who had spotted an opportunity that she believed had potential. Whether it was the thrill of moving to a foreign country or the adventure of a start-up, she jumped right in and backed herself to 'figure it out'. 'Once you decide that your career is very high in terms of priority, everything else falls in place,' she says.

Falguni, like the rest of us, faced her share of challenges in balancing work and life. In fact, she has raised twins while working in London and the US. Her husband, Sanjay Nayar, is a successful professional and runs the India office of a large American global investment company. Falguni admits that when family and friends make demands on her time and attention, it is awkward, and she frequently has to turn them down because of prior commitments. The ones she declines are amply made up for at more convenient times or in some other manner, she says. The ability to say 'no' nicely can be a huge asset for a busy professional woman who needs to use her time wisely. This firm focus on what is important to you is a trait I have seen in many successful people, both men and women.

Falguni says she always made clear to her family her ambition at every stage, so that she set the right expectations. Knowing what you want is the first and most crucial step, but articulating and making it known to people at home and work is just as important. A passion or ambition that goes unrealized because of fear that others may not approve or support you is as tragic as talent that fails to achieve its true potential. In an attempt to keep everyone around them happy, which is in any case an impossible goal, young women often sacrifice their own dreams.

* * *

Ritu Mohanty is an architect and urban planner in her forties, who, after graduating from the school of architecture in Anand, went to Columbia University for a master's degree in urban design. Moving from a small town in Gujarat to an Ivy League school in the US was an audacious move, especially for a girl in the early 2000s. Interestingly, Ritu was accepted by three colleges in the US. Two other colleges were willing to give her admission as well as financial aid, but she chose the one without aid as it was considered the top-ranking college to study urban design. Credit goes to Ritu's parents who have always encouraged their daughters to settle for nothing but the best. While the course lasted only a year, Ritu realized that if you wanted to be a top-notch urban planner, you had to be in New York. Armed with a glowing recommendation from one of her professors, she made it to the top firm specializing in urban design in New York, and spent an entire decade there. India, in those days, did not offer opportunities in urban planning, and most women architects anyway opted for the easier route of interior decoration. Marriage and family came later for Ritu, when she was in her mid-thirties but by then, her career was already on a strong foundation. Ritu's father was an HR professional with an MNC who actively sought out similar opportunities for his other daughter too. She is a successful finance professional working in Switzerland. Her mother, who had to give up her teaching career to raise a family, supported her daughters in their ambition to pursue their careers. She did not give in to societal pressures of having them tie the knot as soon as they came of age. Ritu now teaches urban design in a Mumbai college, a vocation she finds immensely rewarding intellectually, and dabbles in consultancy projects as well.

Shubha Lal is a young entrepreneur whose venture, your-space, sets up hostels for college students. The business that was set up in 2016 started small, but just as it was beginning to take off, love blossomed in Shubha's life. While the families on both sides were very excited to get them married, Shubha decided that her business was at a crucial stage and required her full attention. Her priority at that point in time was clear. Her partner supported this choice and took on a corporate job while she pursued her dreams. They got married a couple of years later.

For a professional, being smart and ambitious means that you don't just let your career drift but navigate it knowingly in the direction that you desire. In an increasingly disruptive world, it is also imperative that you make the right strategic moves.

Maliha is a finance professional who has worked in the energy sector for many years. When she and her husband moved abroad, she consciously opted for a green energy job though all her experience had been in black energy. 'That is where the future is,' she figured.

'Be conscious of your career rather than falling into the next role and the next role,' suggests Tejasvi Ravi. She feels that thinking about where you would like to be can help you feel as though you're moving in the right direction, even if you are going through a bad phase.

Self-awareness and analysis of one's strengths and weaknesses help us in making smarter career moves. A useful framework to follow while planning one's career involves a Venn diagram consisting of three circles. The first one should list your top skills, the second one must have all the roles or job functions that you think you will enjoy doing, while the last one must list jobs that will advance your career. In short, the intersection of the three circles will be the sweet spot between what you are good at, what motivates you and where opportunities lie. If there is nothing in common, it means that you need to add on skills that will qualify you for exciting jobs in the future. Since your skills and interests can change with time, it is a good idea to do this exercise every few years. It is quite normal to not be sure of what your strengths are. In that case, check with people who know you well and are familiar with your work, but make sure that they give you honest feedback.

It is possible that many women don't plan too far ahead as their destinies are tied to that of their husbands and much depends on the assignments or jobs that the husband chooses. Becoming a trailing spouse without actively considering the impact it has on your career can be disastrous. You could end up taking on an assignment that isn't challenging; doesn't do justice to your expertise or experience; or worse still, not find any work at all. Several of the successful women I spoke with chose not to join their husbands on transfers as their own careers were at a crucial or exciting stage.

Being good at functional skills is great, but in order to grow, you need to be able to see the big picture as well. Often it appears that women do a fabulous job of their current assignment but are not very good at planning the next move. They are more process-oriented than goal-oriented. Most women I spoke with said that success, in their view, was being excellent at what they are doing at the current moment. This most certainly means that their focus is on the here and now, and not on the long term. Marshal Goldsmith and Sally Helgesen in their book *How Women Rise* actually suggest that if you are too happy in your current job, you may not be considered for a promotion. While I wouldn't agree with that completely, I think having a slightly longer-term view, and not just being absorbed in the present, would help you plan your career better. Dreaming of being CEO one day, heading a firm or starting your own venture could help a person stay motivated since the goal is in sight. Voicing your dreams makes those around you realize how serious you are about your career and that you have plans for yourself.

While investment banker Kanchan Jain attributes much of her success to the support she got from her family, she has also made some prudent career choices. When her kids were young, she chose London over Hong Kong as her base.

'You could do day trips to most cities in Europe, but work-related travel in South-east Asia was invariably a two to three-day affair,' she reckoned. That made it easier for her and her husband to manage their calendars so that one parent could always be in town for the children. As the children are grown up now, she spends the week in London and the weekend in Gurugram.

Kanchan says she always opted for the best opportunity and felt cheated in assignments where the work was not challenging enough. Whenever there was a choice to be made, her husband also pushed her to prioritize work. Kanchan moved to Korea alone, an assignment that was essential for her to take up the job in London, where the family eventually moved.

While earlier, it was assumed that, more often than not, women would turn down transfers, millennials seem far more open to long-distance relationships.

I asked my unmarried son, a millennial himself (and an entrepreneur with three jobs and a previous venture behind him), if women of his generation would be comfortable taking a back seat and compromising their careers because of marriage or a relationship.

'If the relationship doesn't work out, it wouldn't be fair to the one taking the back seat, right?' is what he said. That reflects today's mindset—far more egalitarian and focused on the self, not to mention wary of relationships, quite unlike those of us who got into marriage thinking it was for keeps.

Subsequently, when I heard the story of twenty-nine-year-old Vandana, a divorcee, I marvelled even further at my son's maturity.

'I had a rather understanding husband when it came to careers. He graduated from a premier B-school, one year after I did. Both of us tried to help each other in our careers. And yes, both salaries were given equal importance. There was one catch, though. Later, when our marriage ran into trouble, I took a sabbatical without any second thoughts. And then I compromised on my role and took up something far from what I loved to save our marriage. Whereas my ex-husband was unwilling to even take a longer vacation from work because he felt it could jeopardize his career. According to him, that was at least one thing that was going well in his life and he didn't wish to mess it up.'

Women are generally known to be good team players, sometimes even harming their own interests in the process. Being smart then, is not about being selfish, but about seeing that in every family decision, your interest is also safeguarded and your career is given adequate priority. Your story will turn out best when you have written your own script!

It appears clear to me that urban Gen Y women are different. They are focused on themselves, surer of what they want and articulate their ambition a lot better. They don't assume that people will understand their dreams. They are not always willing to give up everything to follow their husbands. Like most women, they are team players but they are clear that the 'I' must not get lost in the 'we'.

Dreams and ambition often require that you don't always go along with the plans that your family has in mind for you. Not everyone is comfortable or confident like Ritu and Shubha to be firm about what they want to do. The luckier ones, like Kanchan and Falguni, find parents, husbands or mentors who are invested in their dreams and are willing to nurture their ambitions. A majority of women are guaranteed to face people who have a view on what they must do and not do at every stage in their life and career. You need both courage and determination along with a thick skin to decide who are the people you need to please, whose opinions you need to value and whether it is important for you to be popular or feel fulfilled.

The Recalibration of Ambition

Goa during the rains is at its most beautiful, and the monsoon of 2017 found us there, if only on work and for a day. Harsha and I had just finished a presentation that had lasted almost two hours, one of a few hundred that we have done over the last two decades. One of the most stimulating parts of our work is that it has given us the opportunity to understand a bit about a wide cross section of businesses. One day we would be speaking to insecure IT managers in their forties, struggling to stay relevant while leading teams of bright twenty-five-year-olds who think they know more than their bosses. On another day it could be a highly successful FMCG company caught napping and missing a major trend while they got overconfident and arrogant because of their earlier successes. Over the years, I have thoroughly enjoyed our conversations with clients who have not only offered deep insights about the challenges that companies face but have also gone on to become good friends in the process. This time, our point of contact was the chief marketing officer (CMO), a bright and confident lady of about thirty-five. It was apparent that she had done very well for herself and, on this occasion, seemed rather pleased that the event had been very well-received.

There was a heavy downpour and as we walked briskly towards lunch, she caught up with me.

'Can I ask you something?' she asked, in a voice which, for the first time, sounded a bit hesitant. I thought she wanted to discuss something about leadership, the topic of our talk. She was, after all, ideal leadership material, as I had already noted.

'How do you manage work and home?' she asked, instead.

She and her equally busy and successful husband were under considerable pressure from both their families about contemplating an addition to the family. She couldn't figure out how she would find time to have a baby, with a busy marketing plan for the next eighteen months already chalked out. It was a classic work-life balance issue that was weighing her down. It is an issue that nags every working couple today, and it was more challenging than any product launch or brand campaign that she had ever handled.

'Even if I become a CEO but I don't have kids, my mother will still not see me as a successful person . . . and my mother's approval is important to me,' she confided.

Research studies have consistently shown that men and women start off their careers with comparable levels of ambition. As marriage and children happen, the idealism of youth makes way for practical realism and women tend to recalibrate their ambition. Typically, this starts happening around the age of thirty-five. Children start requiring more attention, spouses become busier in their careers and parents are not as young as they used to be. There is no shying away from the fact that in most societies, women continue to be the primary (and often sole) homemakers and caregivers. You can focus on your career wholeheartedly only when you have the peace of mind that comes with an efficiently run home and reliable care for your young kids or aged parents. Work-life balance is therefore the stepping stone, sort of prerequisite to a successful career. With professional lives being as demanding as they are, work-life balance is not merely about managing time during a hectic period, but an ongoing and constantly evolving exercise to achieve a state of equilibrium.

Undoubtedly, achievement comes with trade-offs, and that could mean giving up hobbies, time for yourself or with your family. Earlier, marriage and kids were assumed to be givens. Increasingly, young women are questioning these assumptions and struggling to find answers, for there are no easy answers. To gain something, you have to let go of something. Leadership requires a lot of time, energy and focus. You need to give undivided attention to your work. A few top women CEOs have homes without functional kitchens; some don't even run their own households, leaving it entirely to the staff. Not all women are comfortable with the idea of completely delegating their home management and feel it is too much of a compromise. If you are like me, you wouldn't like a unidimensional life. My Twitter handle says that I wear multiple hats—a professional, a writer, an amateur keyboard player, a sudoku enthusiast and a homemaker. I love all my hats.

Years of social conditioning have created the notion that a working woman must be an indifferent homemaker and a negligent mother. So often I see professional women fall prey to this imagery and try hard to prove it wrong. They are constantly apologetic for fear that they may appear inadequate on the home front. While that may not be true, one must be realistic about the tasks one can perform. When you spend so much time doing a great job at work, there is no way you can also throw the best parties at home or bake the best chocolate brownies as someone else does. My observation is that winners are clear about their priorities as well as their limitations. They learn to let go of what is not important to them and they are not hard on themselves about what they are not good at. A lot of energy is unnecessarily spent in trying to please everyone and being better than the others at everything.

One of my friends, a few years younger than me, is in a fairly senior position with an IT firm. She has spent most of her working life with the same firm; she had even taken foreign transfers with them when her husband moved. One day, as some of us sat around and talked about what's next for us in our careers, I asked her about moving to the next level. 'That is too much hard work,' she confessed. Their family of four was spread across three continents, her children were not yet independent, so a career plateau seemed a less stressful option to her.

Young Aishwarya is doing very well in the M&A (mergers and acquisitions) practice of a Big 4 accountancy firm. Work excites her and though she loves what she does, she is sceptical if she will ever head the practice one day. She says that in her line of work, rules and regulations change every day and you need to be on top of your game at all times. Since having a family is a priority for her and the top job can be really demanding, Aishwarya is not sure if she will make it to the corner office.

Indeed, leadership is a lot of hard work, and a number of women feel burnt out by the time they get to menopause. We don't realize how much unseen energy we have spent planning birthday parties, coordinating hobby classes and attending to family matters while having full-time jobs and an efficiently run home! Those who harbour dreams of running organizations need to be aware of pacing their innings and conserving energy till the end.

Feeding Your Dreams

Ambition among a majority of women comes tinged with a hint of lament. Chances that could not be grabbed, regrets about opportunities that could not be embraced, breaks that they were worthy of but went to a less deserving man and so on. While getting admission to top-ranking institutes in any field in India is tough by any standard, women who manage to qualify find it harder to stay the course and make it to the top of their profession. But recalibration need not always be downward, and there is a growing number of hugely inspiring stories of women who did not give up on their aspirations.

What I have found common among successful people is that they don't let disappointments bog them down. Instead, they create new opportunities for themselves, fuel their passion and channelize their ambition to actually drive it upward.

Some discover their passion late in their careers, some keep it alive by pivoting their careers and some find novel ways to grow it. You will also find that many of them have had the benefit of encouragement from bosses and mentors or have worked for supportive organizations that nurtured their talent, helped them navigate the difficult phases and backed them to fulfil their dreams.

My own story is a strange one of constraints amidst what seemed a very privileged life. Mine was an unusual career graph that was the result of being denied many regular options and which involved creating opportunities where none existed. My husband Harsha, who was my batchmate in IIMA, was madly in love with cricket, even on campus, and always dreamt of staying connected with the sport. Around the age of nineteen, when he realized that his playing career had plateaued at the university level, he began to dabble in freelance cricket commentary. A degree in engineering followed by an MBA seemed to be a safer option to him and his middle-class Maharashtrian parents. Even while at IIMA, he did a couple of commentary stints on radio and television, but there was no opportunity (or even a thought) of making a career out of it. His broadcasting career took off only around 1993–94, by which time we had two children. It seemed like a one-in-a-million chance and also a dream come true for him, and there was no way we were going to let it pass. He made a tremendous success of his new career and there has been no question of returning to a corporate career. It is a life and career that is very high profile and privileged but also very demanding and requires him to travel for several weeks at a stretch, multiple times in a year. That, for me, has meant less support at home, almost like being a single parent at most times. I have tried every option to ensure that I worked throughout—working flexitime, part-time and working out of home for several years, much before these terms became part of corporate lingo. I have always had to create opportunities for myself, and that required a lot of grit as also creativity.

With a background in statistics and having done courses on quantitative methods, I was ideally suited for a career in market research. In the mid-eighties, when I started my career, only large organizations had the capability to buy and run statistical software. This was way before personal computers came on the scene, when only large companies could afford mainframes. Working for a large organization meant working full-time, and as I said earlier, that option was not available to me while my children were growing up. I spent many years doing qualitative research instead of quantitative research, only because it was more manageable. I vividly recall the few amusing times when there was no option but to take my son to a group discussion, with field staff looking after the toddler while I went about my business. It was not the ideal way to go about work, but then we got by. Being an introvert, I wasn't a natural when it came to group discussions, which require you to get strangers to give free and frank views about various products and services. You need to establish a connection with them within minutes and win their trust so that they are happy to share their candid views. I soon realized that being genuine and committed was enough to build a rapport even with random groups of people, and I slowly and steadily became pretty good at the job.

I remember a particularly funny incident where my research was to be a significant input for a go/no-go decision in the launch of a Gujarati newspaper. We had lined up ten groups of Gujarati readers from different age groups. Gujarati is not a language I speak, so the discussions were in Hindi. After the initial small talk, I asked the first group what was the first thing they read in the morning newspaper. Imagine my shock when the unanimous reply was 'Obituaries!' I was totally zapped when each of the groups threw up the same response. A useful consumer insight was that there is a tremendous social bonding within different Gujarati communities, and when someone from the community expires, a large turnout is expected. Folks need to plan their day around community funerals. Now that made total sense. As a matter of fact, in those days, the Obit section in their papers was huge and some brands promoted it as a free service.

Every assignment added to my confidence, and I found that I was good with even really personal products. Good enough for clients to call me up for projects years after I had moved on to other ventures. I have tried every trick in the book to keep my career afloat, and with every experience I have learnt new skills, developed a great network and built a reputation for myself.

About two decades ago, Harsha and I started conducting workshops on 'The Winning Way—Learnings from Sport for Managers', where we combined our skills as well as knowledge. It was a unique programme and we got many more requests than we could handle. No such genre existed and at around 600 sessions at last count, it is the only speaking series in the country that has been running for over two decades. We worked around Harsha's cricket calendar and had to turn down numerous requests when they clashed with his schedule. Despite the tremendous success of the programme and the book that we wrote based on our talks, I realized that, being a live programme, it could not be scaled beyond a point and that I would have to find another channel for my growing restlessness. In 2011, I started Bizpunditz, a video-learning library for managers. Again, it was the first venture of its kind in the country and I managed to build it to a significant size and sell it to a large edtech platform at the end of 2020.

We use a line in 'The Winning Way': 'Don't let what you cannot do interfere with what you can do.'

This has been my motto all my life and I believe it works for everyone, whatever your situation. I had enough constraints and excuses to sit back and enjoy a comfortable life but chose to devote my life to create two impactful businesses. Neither venture had anything to do with my initial training in quantitative methods and subsequent experience in advertising and marketing, but they are proof that, with some innovative thinking and a lot of hard work, you can give yourself a reasonable shot at success.

Roopa Kudva is a name that is bound to come up in a list of the top ten influential women in Indian business. Roopa was MD and CEO of the ratings company CRISIL before going on to head the investment firm, Omidyar Network India. Despite her phenomenal success, Roopa believes that even at CRISIL, she was not the smartest person around and attributes her success to sheer hard work and smart career moves.

Roopa talks about the time she was offered a posting in Paris, one that she accepted without batting an eyelid.

'Wouldn't you want to go home and discuss it with your husband?' she was asked.

Roopa was confident that it was a great opportunity and there was no way her husband Vivek would object. As it happened, Roopa believes that Paris was the turning point in her career. Till then, she hadn't been very ambitious. She had kept following her husband in all his postings, even sticking to a company that gave her the flexibility to move to every new city that her husband moved to.

'Till Paris, I had a worm's eye view of things. Paris enabled me to get a view from the outside, a bird's-eye view,' she says.

This was the move she required to step into a leadership position. On her return, while she was at an offsite, she surprised herself by approaching her boss and mentor, then CEO of CRISIL, Ravimohan, with a hastily-put-together, three-slide presentation.

'CRISIL needs a chief ratings officer,' it said. She went on to tell him why she would be the right person for that job. Very rarely have I found women like Roopa who are so clear about what they want and go after it.

Despite a large number of women opting to study medicine, women surgeons are hard to find. Dr Anita Patel is a urologist with a Fellowship of the Royal College of Surgeons (FRCS)—the first and perhaps only woman in the country with an FRCS in urology and a *sangeet visharad* to boot! Early in her career, she realized that there was a unique space that she could carve out for herself. In India, you had paediatricians and you had urologists, but no one had expertise in both. She worked towards creating a largely self-learnt niche, even doing pro bono work till she gained the experience. She is now considered the last word on the evaluation of paediatric bladders for various diseases, all over the country.

Good organizations provide training to their managers and ensure that they grow and learn. Self-employed folks like doctors, lawyers, architects and entrepreneurs don't have the benefit of planned training programmes. Anita says it is very common for a doctor to get into a comfort zone and stop growing. Once you have gained experience, routine practice gets into cruise control, she feels. To override this challenge, Anita invests in herself by giving talks and presentations at conferences, often offering her own inputs to the organizers. She says she keeps a close eye on feedback and would be upset if her session did not figure in the top few. If you have the desire to grow and improve, you can always find ways to power that hunger.

Even at this stage in her career, Rama Bijapurkar thinks about how not to get complacent or irrelevant. She agrees to take on unfamiliar assignments with stretch deadlines that force her to get the job done and also build knowledge in the process. Pushing your limits and then backing yourself to deliver, she believes, is a sure way to keep growing. Ever so often, you find women harping on about their limitations or lack of experience, too scared to step out of their comfort zone.

In many ways it is still a man's world, so it pays to think like one, at least from time to time. There is really so much that we can learn from men that in certain tough or pressure situations, it is a good idea to pause and think what a man would do in the same situation. I don't know if it is their genetic wiring or just the advantage that they have in sheer numbers but the average man seems to have far fewer inhibitions, a lot more self-confidence and better networking abilities than the average woman. There is, however, nothing to say that these traits cannot be learnt through observation and deliberate practice.

If your ambition is way ahead of your current reality, staying within your comfort zone will not help you get there.

Professional growth comes from putting yourself in unfamiliar territory, accepting challenging assignments and surrounding yourself with people who are not quite like you. I wasn't surprised at all when Anita Sanghi told me how, right since her early days, she had volunteered for stretch assignments that involved global, multilocation teams. 'When you work for an MNC, you need to network globally, not just in your familiar home office,' she says. Later in her career, when it was time for her to move into top management, and candidates were selected for promotion based on the number of votes from global colleagues, she was the one selected, as she was a known name because of the projects that she had contributed to. The network pays off in many interesting ways but first you need to invest in it.

Rishi Gour is CEO of Theobroma and has worked extensively in global organizations. He agrees with Anita that networking in your home country is not enough when you work for large MNCs. You need to be visible to influential colleagues from overseas as they can prove to be good sponsors when it comes to applying for global positions. Rishi believes that there is some amount of subjectivity when it comes to filling a role. Typically, there is one person who takes the call but four or five other people who influence the decision. Getting to know the people who are truly influential is important to one's success in a multinational, he feels.

Winning against all odds can be the theme of Arpita's life. Arpita is one of four sisters from an Odia family. She made her way to IIT Kharagpur to study instrumentation engineering, without even attending a coaching class. She then appeared for the Common Admission Test (CAT) and got interview calls to all IIMs, except IIMA. What a phenomenal achievement by any standards! And then, since the family put immense pressure on her to get married, she had to abandon the idea of doing an MBA with a heavy heart.

The story doesn't end there. Her dream to study in an IIM never deserted her, so marriage and a kid later, and this time with more support on the home front, Arpita joined the Post Graduate Programme in Management for Executives (PGPX) programme at IIMA and made it to the dean's list. Continuing with her unusual choices, she works in the male-dominated oil and gas sector in a business development role.

Arpita's determination and courage brings me back to Falguni's formula of being ziddi. Keeping your dream alive is the surest way to staying the course.

There is no denying, though, that Arpita managed to fulfil her dream the second time around because she had more support at home. The confidence to dream rides on the wings of support from the family. Those who are not confident about familial backing are afraid to spell out their dreams for fear that they might find disapproval and their dreams will remain unfulfilled. Women who harbour aspirations are still a minority, which makes it essential that their ambitions be spelt out loud and clear. Dreaming aloud is about getting on board those who believe in your potential and your ambition and are willing to support you in this journey. The journey is demanding, involves sacrifices and adjustments from you as well as those around you and can be difficult without a buy-in from them.

For us, family support came in the form of a conveniently located flat that my parents owned and generously allowed us to use. Mumbai can be a hard city for those without a home and could require them to live in the distant suburbs. Being spared the long commute, we saved time, money and energy, and that was probably what allowed Harsha to chase his dreams. Unfortunately, neither my parents nor we could afford another house in Mumbai, so my parents moved to Pune, leaving me with no support from either side of the family. While life has been more than kind to us, I do wonder sometimes how my career would have turned out had they been around to help out.

Navigating Speed Breakers

Marriage and children will always remain the two biggest speed breakers in a woman's career. Home and kids can potentially distract and make single-minded focus on the career a challenge.

For all the progress we have made with increasing the number of professionally qualified women, when it comes to marriage, the parents' thought process is still pretty traditional, especially in smaller towns and less affluent families.

'Girl child, twenty-eight, unmarried. This is what my mother's hypertension diagnosis reads like!' says Sona, one of my respondents. She is an IIM graduate and works for an MNC. A bright career is ahead of her, but the issue of marriage is currently overshadowing her whole life.

'It just amazes me that you might be an achiever in all other aspects but for a family or society at large, there's something terribly wrong if you are a Miss and not a Mrs. Your family just starts doubting if the "freedom and unconditional support" has "spoilt" you to the extent that you don't wish to conform to the societal standards of marriage by the age of twenty-five or twenty-six. The same family that once taught me to not care about societal norms pertaining to a girl child, like not going out or doing the household chores and instead building a career for yourself, wants me to tick this M box as soon as possible!'

Marriage continues to remain the biggest milestone for most women. The idea of marriage enters a girl's mind and conscience way before she even starts thinking of a career. Society discusses it, parents plan for it and Bollywood makes it look like the ultimate fantasy! Every Indian knows that 'settling down' for a girl refers to getting married, not becoming financially independent or buying a home. If girls remain unmarried till twenty-seven or twenty-eight, the family starts getting desperate. Even girls who are brought up being told that education and career are most important, start feeling let down by parents who suddenly start behaving as if not getting married on time or finding the right match is some sort of failure, no matter how well you might be doing in your career. Once the marriage is fixed, they shy away from telling the groom and his family how bright and ambitious their daughter is for fear that it might upset the alliance. The daughter's marriage still gets a significantly higher priority than her career. A wasted career causes much less regret; a failed marriage carries a much bigger stigma.

If marriage puts an end to pressure tactics from parents, it brings with it expectations from the in-laws. We may not see much of this in the big cities where couples earn enough to be able to afford an independent home and fairly expensive house help. But in smaller cities, within traditional joint families, the women are expected to carry most of the load of running the home. The same families that insist on an 'educated bahu' have no idea of the demands on a professional working woman. Today's career women, just like men, need to work long hours, stay connected 24/7, travel at short notice, attend work-related events after office hours and invest in their careers by attending courses or studying online. Our society is at a stage where many women who are mothers-in-law now have had jobs but not careers. There is a tendency among such women when they become mothers or mothers-in-law to taunt and say that they too were working women but managed both fronts well, little realizing that there is a huge difference between jobs and careers. No wonder then that youngsters prefer to live on their own these days.

'In a patriarchal society, women know the side effects of ambition even before they know ambition,' says Harkirat Bedi, who passed out of IIM Lucknow in 2015 and works for an MNC. Harkirat herself was lucky to have parents who supported her to go backpacking alone in Eastern Europe when she was twenty-four, the age at which her cousins were getting married. Not everyone is as lucky as her, she feels, but is happy to see society changing slowly. While women are becoming ambitious, there is also the expectation that they remain 'family-oriented'. Ambition is now more easily accepted but it comes with terms and conditions attached, which is probably what is meant by parents being supportive of a girl's career but not ambitious about her success. It is all about how long you can keep the career ball in the air while ensuring that you don't drop any of the other balls.

Of all the various decisions that a woman makes at various stages in her life, the single most important choice, one that affects many other decisions, is the choice of spouse. I guess it is important to a man as well, but not with such far-reaching implications to his career.

A supportive husband, a fellow professional from a related field, could be her entry pass to a much wider social and professional network. He could be a sounding board while taking key career decisions or a shock absorber who understands her work pressures. So often you hear women credit their husbands with being the wind beneath their wings. It is truly heart-warming to see husbands who are happy to encourage their wives to forge ahead.

An increasingly realistic scenario these days is that the woman earns more than the man. Even in the twenty-first century, it is a difficult situation for the fragile male ego to handle. I see parents of high achieving daughters worry about such possibilities. They fear that success at work could lead to failure in the marriage as not too many men are comfortable with the idea of a more successful wife.

This was an issue that was weighing on the minds of at least two sets of parents at our thirty-fifth IIMA batch reunion. It is interesting to observe how every few years the most discussed topics in the group keep changing. At this event, careers and achievements took a back seat, and getting children married and having grandchildren dominated the discussions. Many from the batch had graduated to becoming in-laws, and those who had daughters were particularly looking forward to the arrival of grandchildren. There were worries as well. Retirement and health issues topped the list. One guy in particular looked terribly stressed, enough for everyone around to notice. Was it his recent retirement, I wondered. Men are known to go through anxiety and depression, if they haven't planned their retirement well. It came as a big surprise to me that it was his very bright and successful daughter who was the cause of his sleepless nights.

Much to the parents' pride, the daughter had majored in finance from a good B-school, graduated with flying colours and joined a well-known consultancy firm. Then somewhere along the way, she fell in love with an HR manager and decided to marry him. The father, having spent all his life in the corporate sector, realized that her career graph looked far more promising than his and advised her against the marriage. The girl, being a millennial, stood her ground and refused to accept. Two years down the line, the father's prognosis rang true and the poor girl found herself in a difficult spot. Luckily for her, the parents are the supportive kind who realize that a divorce is far better than a bad marriage.

* * *

Ruth Bader Ginsburg was an American lawyer and jurist who served as an associate justice of the Supreme Court of the United States from 1993 until her death in September 2020. Best known for her legal battles dismantling gender discrimination, Ruth's own love story may be the best case study for proving the power of an egalitarian partnership. That Ruth supported her husband Marty Ginsberg comes as no surprise at all, but it was clear that Ruth would never have achieved the iconic success that she did without the support of Marty. Here was a man who ranked his wife's career equal to his own. Marty offered Ruth complete support at a professional as well as personal level. Not only did he run a tireless campaign supporting her nomination to the Supreme Court but as spouse of a Supreme Court Justice, he played his role as well as any wife would have. Famously, he baked cakes for her clerks and hosted dinners, for which he himself cooked.

In a note that he wrote to Ruth just before his death in 2010, he said, 'What a treat it has been to watch you progress to the very top of the legal world.'

Every Ruth truly deserves a Marty! In reality, however, while we find many Ruths around, there are very few Martys. So, while finding a Marty might seem like a tall order, one can at least ensure that we stay clear of those who think that if the man earns enough, there is no need for the woman to pursue her career.

While the romantic notion of being swept off your feet when you fall in love may suggest that love is blind, modern-day wisdom recommends that you go into it with your eyes wide open and leave nothing to chance. Your heart may go aflutter but don't forget to consult the head. There is a good chance your dreams could rest on the choice you make.

'Conversations' is a word that crops up frequently when I speak to women around thirty. They realize it is important they have a conversation with the prospective spouse and his family about their ambition, how serious they are about their careers, the demands that their careers are likely to make and so on. It helps them understand the expectations of his family as well. Will they be expected to dress a certain way, will they have to apologize in case they stay late at the workplace, will they have social obligations like observing fasts, performing poojas, etc.? This is just as important in love marriages as it is in arranged marriages since the views of the family may be quite different from those of the groom. I was taken aback when a young IIM graduate who married a colleague told me that she had to wear a *ghoonghat* in front of her in-laws!

Once a marriage is fixed, much time and energy is spent discussing the wedding ceremony, coordinating the outfits, the sangeet and the video shooting, when in fact the emphasis should be on discussing the young couple's dreams, aspirations, attitudes and expectations.

As love marriages become more common, it would make sense for women to have conversations around 'what if' scenarios—what if she earns more than him, who looks after his/her parents in case they need looking after, on what basis would you agree to relocate and other such things. Young women today are clear about their need for financial autonomy; they want to be equal partners in sharing expenses and contributing to buying a house. As more women pursue careers, they need support from parents, and often it is the girl's parents who chip in. I have had many young women tell me that they would like to contribute to the home so that their parents can enjoy equal status in the house. This is again a typically Indian issue and one that women feel strongly about.

I was once having a conversation with someone who runs a marriage bureau and was amused when he told me that they held group discussions for prospective brides and grooms on such topics. When I thought about it, I realized that this was a subtle as well as a progressive way of understanding mindsets of prospective spouses and shortlisting those who matched your wavelength!

You will find that women in their thirties and forties, unlike their mothers' generation, are taking charge of their own lives. Unlike previous generations where women's choices got dictated by constraints, here is a generation that is driven by opportunity. Whether it is a marriage proposal or a promotion, they are not coy. Having set their minds on something or someone, they are willing to go after it and make it happen.

Having a child can be a career-threatening decision for many, and yet most women cannot imagine a life without children. If looked at dispassionately, not having children is the easiest and most logical solution to be able to focus on your career unhindered. Yet, none of the mothers I interviewed felt that it would have been a worthwhile trade-off for more success in their careers.

Women whose careers are going well naturally postpone having a child till their mid-thirties. Advancing age coupled with the stress of work (and travel in many cases), for both the partners means that conception becomes another high-pressure project with a deadline, one that has slim chances of success.

'Till about ten to fifteen years ago, the trend was for women to have children fairly early and that meant balancing career-building and motherhood together. This was tough unless there was a huge support system of parents, in-laws and a husband who stepped up to share the home responsibilities. Home and children got prioritized for the women who then got a chance to focus on their careers only after the kids had grown up. That made women late-starters or non-starters,' says executive coach Promila Ayyangar. She finds that today's trend of marrying late or having children late ensures that the mothers are older and more mature and as a result, surer about where they want to take their careers. In a fast-changing world particularly, a career break has more far-reaching consequences and needs to be thought through very carefully. 'Too long a break often ends up being the end of the road for women who can feel disconnected and no longer qualified for the job they left behind. The bigger challenge is to get an employer to give them an opportunity and believe in them—that they can learn and deliver and be trusted to be serious about their career,' she feels.

Society still believes that men work to support the family while women work for themselves, so when a woman, even a professionally qualified woman, quits her career, there is minimal stigma or guilt attached. Lack of a good enough support system at home is the single biggest reason for women to quit their full-time jobs. While the more resourceful ones manage to keep their careers alive by working part-time or freelance, a large number are forced to put a full stop to work. Work-life balance really started becoming an issue when women with careers were required to spend long hours at work. That means that the rest of the family has to chip in with the work that otherwise would fall into the lap of stay-at-home moms. It comes as no surprise that in households that are fairly comfortable financially, a non-working mother becomes a convenient and comfortable option for all, including the woman herself. Often, any complaint or even comment from a working woman about being pulled in different directions or the need for a break is met with the familiar refrain, 'Why do you need to work?' suggesting that if there is no financial compulsion, a woman is better off at home. It does not even cross their minds that a career has more to do with her sense of identity, not merely income.

I am not sure in what context Catherine Zeta-Jones said, 'Whether your pregnancy was meticulously planned, medically coaxed or happened by surprise, one thing is certain, your life will never be the same.'

But it cannot be denied that a maternity break can set a woman's career back, at least in the short run. Notwithstanding the now generous paid leave of six months, the problems still remain. Despite planning your return to work meticulously, you could still have challenges at work. Your team could have changed, your role might have been given to someone else or you might be getting into a new project midway. All these can be unnerving and could leave you a bit rattled. There is also the ticklish bit about losing out on part of your bonus or increment or even being denied a promotion. While it is true that your colleagues were busy working while you chose to take a break to have a child, it is still upsetting if you have to report to someone who was at the same level as you or even a junior. You might even get the feeling that you can hear your dreams shattering. Remind yourself that there will always be opportunities to catch up if you show patience and positivity and are determined to do well.

Certain organizations are doing their bit by following best practices in performance ratings when it comes to maternity leave by taking the average of the previous three years. That seems very fair. Interestingly, public sector undertakings (PSUs) and the government along with many MNCs are seen to be good employers when it comes to guarding women's interests. As K. Ramkumar, who used to be executive director at ICICI Bank and also head of their HR, puts it, 'Maternity leave is not a "benefit". It needs to be designed into the system as a design parameter. It cannot be held against the person. It is a cost that needs to be built into the business.'

Ramkumar gives several examples of women in ICICI Bank who returned from maternity leave to settle back comfortably at work. Many of them went on to head various companies in the ICICI group. In banking, there are positions like branch heads that cannot be left vacant for long periods. In roles where it is possible for the woman to return, the question they ask is whether you have developed a good deputy to run the function when you are not there. Training and empowering the deputy to take over if and when the need arises is a great HR policy anyway, as it helps with leadership development for the entire organization.

Hindustan Unilever Limited (HUL) is also committed to increasing their efforts to ensure that women managers don't fall off the corporate ladder due to want of support. Apart from their numerous policy initiatives, they have even tried a tie-up with various partners like ProEves and Portea that offer day care and nursing care at home to provide employees with a reliable network of support. While this service was made available to all employees, male and female, it was one way to make it less stressful for women while returning from maternity leave. Anuradha Razdan, executive director, HR at HUL, says, 'Our insight has been that women tend to leave because they don't feel adequately supported at work. Hence, over the last few years, we have made a concerted effort to listen to what our female employees have to say and have been providing tailored flexibility and opportunities to upskill upon return, leading to a very successful maternity return rate of 97 per cent.'

It is heartening to know that this year, Unilever has reached a fifty-fifty split across all managerial roles globally. If we want more women to stay the course and prevent the leadership pipeline from leaking, we will need many more companies to be supportive of women's dreams.

Not all employers are that committed to inclusive practices. Women back from maternity leave might find that teams and organizations have moved on while they were away and that nobody really missed them. That is again not very easy to swallow, especially if you had been very dedicated, so don't forget to carry the thick skin along when you decide to rejoin!

Jagriti was a top sales and marketing performer in the MNC that she worked for. Her commitment was such that she worked till two days before her baby was born and travelled as long as the doctor permitted. When she shared the news of her maternity break with line managers, her rating and related bonus were immediately impacted, despite overachieving on all objective parameters on the Key Performance Indicator (KPI) sheet.

Upon returning to a marketing role and requesting flexibility on travel for a couple of months while she was nursing her child, she saw that the boss lacked empathy and understanding of the support a young mother needs, making her comeback very stressful, with expectations of extended travel and late hours at work.

'It was as if, for the organization, the moment I was pregnant, I was not talent any more,' laments Jagriti. While most women don't word it as strongly as she does, many suspect that once women have kids, many organizations stop considering them for important roles even long after their need for some flexibility is over. Organizations that value talent, both male and female, can be great enablers for careers while those with a poor work culture can leave even their star employees disgruntled.

Having said that, bearing children is a choice that we make, and like all other choices, there will be consequences and trade-offs. Taking ownership of your choice and seeing how best you can manage your career having made that choice is the smartest way to ensure success and happiness.

Dreaming aloud and letting your seniors know about how you would like to plan your career path will give them an idea of your determination to stay on track.

Where Are You on the Ambition Scale?

Sudhir Sitapati's book on Hindustan Unilever is called *The CEO Factory*. A large number of managers who were trained at HUL have gone on to become CEOs of other companies. Sudhir talks about the role of organizational values and culture in the success of an organization. He believes that one of the reasons that Unilever internationally, and HUL in India, have managed to remain at the top of their game for the last six decades is their commitment to their values of Action, Care, Courage and Truth. With diversity and inclusion becoming an integral part of their corporate agenda, Unilever says they have reached a 50:50 gender balance across their management levels. What remains to be seen is how many women CEOs emerge from this thriving factory.

For a long time, the honour of being the CEO factory for women in finance has gone to Industrial Credit and Investment Corporation of India (ICICI). Kalpana Morparia, Lalita Gupte, Shikha Sharma, Renuka Ramnath, Chanda Kochhar, Madhabi Puri Buch, Zarine Daruwala, Vishakha Mulye and Vedika Bhandarkar were all products of ICICI who went on to become CEOs of various financial organizations. Through most of these years, Ramkumar has headed HR at ICICI. He has had a ringside view of both the organization and the women who went on to become success stories.

'There are three categories of women,' starts Ramkumar. The first category, he says, are ambitious women who are not afraid of broadcasting their ambition. They deal with whatever challenges they encounter and don't expect the organization to solve their problems. They pursue their ambition knowing full well that not much support is likely to come their way. Conversations regarding the ecosystem don't occur to them. Most of the women just mentioned fall in the first category.

'The remarkable ICICI women were achievers. They asked for no privileges or dispensations. All they wanted was a fair and equitable system which was a meritocracy. ICICI provided it for them and all its employees,' he emphasizes.

Ramkumar can recount several examples of how the feisty women neither asked for any concessions nor were treated any differently. In ICICI, if teams ran into a major problem, there would be a closed-door brainstorming session where no one from the team went home till the problem was solved. No exception was made for anyone, regardless of their seniority or gender.

Ramkumar tells a particularly amusing story of a time when, as a mid-level manager, he and his colleagues worked several late nights trying to chase a deadline but ran into a technical issue. Realizing that there was a chance of missing the deadline, around midnight he called up Kalpana Morparia who was the manager then and told her about the problem. At around 2 a.m., Ram thought he saw Kalpana, dressed in a blue salwar kameez walking towards the team. He was convinced he was hallucinating. Not only was he hungry and majorly sleep-deprived but he had never seen Kalpana in a salwar kameez. She always wore a saree to work. He had to pinch himself before it sank in that she had indeed driven to the office at that hour to help the team resolve the issue.

The second category, according to Ramkumar, consists of women who are ambitious but don't articulate it. They fear that other people might disapprove. Their bigger fear is that if they don't make it to the level they aspire to, they would have egg on their face. These women believe that there is a male network that they would need help to break into. They realize that there are many disadvantages in the system and expect someone to intervene and make it a more level playing field.

The third category of women, says Ramkumar, is ambitious up to a point in their lives. Often with outstanding talent, they break away due to domestic considerations. When the compulsion disappears and they have an opportunity to re-enter, they find that they have changed as people. A cushy life at home and a comfortable financial situation are often enough to take your focus away from your professional commitments. Opportunities to re-enter exist, thinks Ramkumar, provided you are a realist. If the break is long, your batchmates and juniors would have moved on and you might need to report to them. This is often not acceptable to women in this category, whereas women from category one, in the same situation, are willing to accept, fight back and bridge the gap at the earliest. Most organizations are now willing to give some amount of credit for past performance but making unrealistic demands like batch parity even after a five-year break makes things difficult for the organization. And as Neha Bagaria of JobsForHer says, 'Reskilling and confidence-building are both required for a smooth and successful return to work.'

Madhabi Puri Buch is the first woman and first person from the private sector to be appointed chairperson of the Securities and Exchange Board of India (SEBI).

In the early 1990s, Madhabi quit her job at ICICI, took her young child and followed her husband when he took up an assignment in the UK. In those days, educational qualifications from India were not recognized abroad. So, despite having passed out of India's no. 1 business school, the only job Madhabi could find was as a salesgirl in a store, which she accepted saying, 'Who knows what I might learn?' When she returned to India, ICICI wanted her back. She was away for about three years, but ICICI graciously gave her credit for almost two. She was grateful for the offer and says that that gesture on the part of ICICI was one of many that made her feel a strong sense of commitment to her employer. Many years later, when she was running customer service for the bank across 1500 branches, she would often refer to her experience as a salesgirl, particularly a poster in her store that said, 'If you don't serve the customer, the competition will.'

In my many conversations that have served as the basis for this book, I have found a few traits that are common to real achievers. One of them is that they are all fair and positive. Successful women never make their struggle a gender issue. They leave their gender behind and go to work as equal employees. They would certainly qualify to be in Ramkumar's first category. Both genders have their own struggles and many organizations make concessions for their women employees. We need to be grateful for such privileges that most responsible employers provide and not treat them as entitlements. To get treated equally, we must first ensure that we deliver our 100 per cent. If we do our jobs well and on time, we don't give anyone a chance to say that we left early or compromised in any manner.

Other than sexual harassment, which is unpardonable, everyone gets their share of petty bosses, disappointments and bias in the workplace. Anita Sanghi believes that one should always speak up against unfair treatment. Those who are not in a position to do so must seek help from those they can trust. She recognizes that being in a senior management role, she is well placed to help others and feels that managers everywhere must show empathy and provide help to those who are not as well placed.

'The world unfortunately isn't fair, and it is important to try and focus on the positives,' says Anita. In her varied assignments, she can think of only one really bad experience with a manager who seemed biased against her. Sometimes, focusing on the positives and trying to be vocal doesn't help—even when it's a powerful woman like Anita. She ended up leaving the organization and landed a fabulous job. 'He was responsible for getting me to move out of my comfort zone, so I actually went and thanked him,' she says. The ability to stay calm and positive is a wonderful trait, especially when life gets tough, and you find the pressure a bit too much to handle.

The spectrum of ambition is very wide and you will find company wherever you are on it. You have to figure out where you will be most comfortable and fulfilled. Comfortable is easy to figure out but fulfilled is equally important for talented and qualified professionals.

Young managers could use Ramkumar's interesting insights of the female mindset to see what category you see yourself in and also learn what you need to do if you want to join the ranks of these leaders who went on to have successful careers.

1) While career paths are not cast in stone, just imagining them can be very motivating. What is your long-term dream? Think of a few short-term goals that will get you there.

2) Think of a situation where 'I' got sacrificed for 'we'. Could you have handled it differently such that both could have been protected?

For a Healthy Career Graph

To have a fulfilling career, work needs to be manageable (it cannot be a burden you can't bear), rewarding (it must stimulate you and you must feel valued) and motivating (you need to have a plan and a future).

So, ask yourself:

- Are you proud of the work you do? Is your family emotionally invested in your career?
- Do you have a career path or long-term goal in mind?
- Have you shared your goal and ambition with your family or organization?
- When you go through a rough patch, does the thought of quitting cross your mind?

- Have you proactively sought out career opportunities?
- Are your career choices largely driven by either convenience or financial considerations?
- Do you look forward to getting to work?
- If you had to give up work, would it make you unhappy? Will your family or your colleagues feel sorry?
- Have you invested in any manner in your career—attended courses or conferences, published papers, joined industry forums?
- Have you organized a good support system that allows you to focus on your career?

Chapter 3

Investing in Yourself

Rama Bijapurkar, marketing consultant and author, has been an inspiration for many generations. Every conversation with Rama is educating and insightful. She is best known for her work in the area of consumer insight, brands and market research. While I am familiar with her work and her writing, I was fascinated when she disclosed that she even sees herself as a brand that gets reflected through her speaking assignments, writing or publishing papers. Interestingly, like all good brand managers, she takes stock of her brand every few years, thinking seriously about her brand positioning and the space she is in. In the middle of her career, she had a discussion with one of her former teachers, Prof. Indira Parikh, and figured that there were hardly any people who had this unusual combination of both business and consumer understanding, like she did. Rama remembers Prof. Parikh's words to her, 'If there is a game only you know how to play, you have to create your own playground for it.' Much of her subsequent work, teaching and writing, understandably have been in that space, a space that she has dominated. Over the last two decades, Rama has been part of many boards and probably has more board experience than any other Indian, man or woman. And this was well before the requirement to have at least one woman on every board became compulsory. 'Was it easy?' I asked her. She admits that initially there were many things she didn't know or understand. But a good teacher is also a good student, so she made a note of whatever she didn't understand and sought help from her 'tuition club'—friends she could learn from.

Quite like Rama, Hyderabad-based Dr Deepa Bhide managed to find a unique niche for herself. Deepa is a gold medallist paediatrician, but marrying into a patriarchal family and having kids early meant that Deepa's career had a slow start. A serious illness at an early age became a further constraint. While she recovered healthwise, Deepa's work life had taken a beating, so she pivoted her career and did a certification in project management. That made her a unique candidate with a dual qualification for the emerging healthcare industry in India. Today, she is a team member of the Ethics Insight Team, a global team for championing ethics of the world-renowned Project Management Institute (PMI). With the children now on their own, Deepa is ready for even bigger challenges. She is a star who managed to find opportunity even in the face of difficulty.

If you are serious about your career, you need to actively take charge of it. It's only when you invest in it that it will reap dividends. As with Rama and Deepa, this is a trait I have found in all those who do well.

Often, we marvel at someone's success and think of how lucky they have been. It is only when you get to hear the backstory that you realize they are no different from the rest of us. They too have had their share of challenges but the manner in which they addressed their issues and found solutions is what sets them apart.

Roopa Kudva, head of Omidyar Network India (who was a year junior to me at IIMA, but a dorm-mate) grew up in Assam, where her father served as an Indian Administrative Service (IAS) officer. Coming from a small town, young Roopa felt she was at a disadvantage in terms of her language skills. Growing up, she regularly listened to the British Broadcasting Corporation (BBC) to improve her English and public-speaking skills. From Assam to IIMA to heading CRISIL, a listed company, it has been one hell of a journey. Roopa is a great believer in the power of hard work and even today, you will never see her turn up unprepared for any engagement.

Hard work is the greatest gift you can give yourself and your career. One of my favourite concepts from *The Winning Way*, my earlier book, is the categorization of people into stretch players and slack players. The belief is that people are born with a certain amount of god-given ability but what they do with that ability depends entirely on the individual's attitude, and that is something that is totally in their own hands. Those who display a great attitude of hard work and discipline make their abilities look far greater than they would otherwise appear and they qualify as stretch players. Slack players, on the other hand, make their abilities appear diminished as a result of poor work ethic. In simple terms, attitude is what makes people overachieve or underperform.

My earliest experience of a stretch player was Neha, my best friend in school. We were thick as thieves and spent many hours doing what we loved most, solving maths problems. Though not a topper, she was hard-working and passionate about maths. When she cleared her chartered accountancy (CA) exams on the first attempt, I was so proud of her achievement! Neha has gone on to hold CFO positions in various organizations. In the first two decades of her career, she stayed with a single, rather conservative organization in the chemicals sector and grew to be the CFO. She was always keen to learn about other roles, not only in finance but also sales, purchase and production. As she put it, she always aspired to be in her boss's circle and wanted to contribute to the larger organization, not just to her own department. Initially her boss, with his traditional mindset, found her enthusiasm odd, but once he saw her keenness to learn, he took her under his wing and gave her enough opportunities and exposure in various forums. Neha's appetite for learning didn't diminish with success and seniority. In one of her roles, she was required to address small groups of people, and she suddenly realized that she didn't have either the skill or the confidence to do it. She promptly joined a toastmasters' club and worked on her communication skills, happily winning several prizes along the way.

Forty-year-old Prerna Bhutani is a recent entrepreneur with a start-up in the haircare space. Before that, for many years, she was in a field where personal positioning mattered a lot.

'Venture capital is an industry that is driven by perception, and how you position yourself makes a huge difference. Being a newbie in the industry, I've faced numerous situations when I was thrust into meetings where I didn't have a clue about what was happening around me. I was bothered by how other people might have perceived me and that affected my confidence. In those situations, I made sure I went back and read about whatever I didn't understand in the meeting so I could do better in the next one. And that always worked.'

There are other ways of investing in yourself, besides hard work. Deepali Naair is the CMO at IBM, India and South Asia, and is a regular on panel discussions and jury panels at conferences. She sees it as an opportunity to demonstrate her skills and grow her knowledge as well as her network. This network has often helped her professionally. Not only does she volunteer for these opportunities but she also offers feedback and suggestions to the organizers. Her helpful nature and involvement result in her being seen as a resource that can be tapped again for future events. Never averse to going back to the classroom, she has spent out of her pocket to do several courses and even hired an executive coach at her own expense.

Are you seeing the pattern there? It's not withdrawing under the pressure of not knowing but instead rising up to face the challenge and finding ways to fill in the gaps. While taking the responsibilities of their growth and learning in their own hands, these women have formed amazing personal and professional networks that they can reach out to whenever they require. This is particularly fascinating since most women I spoke with admitted that they were either no good at it in the beginning or didn't enjoy it at all. It is clearly a skill that can be acquired.

Visibility is essential in today's world where out of sight quickly becomes out of mind. Your social media profile is your new calling card. In the gig economy, your personal brand will be everything. So those of you who have stayed clear of LinkedIn and Twitter, start working on your personal brand right away. For solopreneurs like lawyers and doctors too, visibility in industry forums and remaining in circulation is important for your brand equity.

Gone are the days when joining the workforce signalled the end of education. The future workplace will require managers to continuously upgrade their skills. The onus of upskilling could well be on the employees themselves, rather than on the organization. Online courses provide easy access to education, and employees are encouraged to complete a number of certifications, especially during lean periods or as preparation for new projects. Learning is, without doubt, the best self-investment, and ambitious people don't lose a single opportunity to learn from formal or informal sources.

The second most common reason for women to give up work is the husband's transfer to another city or country. Being a trailing spouse can often mean taking a career break since many countries don't automatically offer an accompanying spouse a work visa. Even in cases where the visa is not an issue, the relocation could mean starting afresh for the spouse, whether it is looking for the right assignment or building a new professional network. However, not all trailing spouses end up becoming ladies of leisure.

Ruchira Chaudhary is the author of the bestseller *Coaching: The Secret Code to Uncommon Leadership*. Her journey to becoming an executive coach is an interesting one since she started off as a management consultant in India and thought of pivoting her career when she followed her husband to Qatar and then Singapore. Though she did not have a job in hand while moving, she used her work network and past association in that geography to land herself some freelance consultancy assignments in Doha, Qatar. I agree with her completely when she says that you need to invest in relationships because you never know where your next job will come from. Encouraged by the response she received to her new line of work, she decided to upskill, and her move to Singapore saw her enrol in the University of Chicago's Booth School of Business Asia campus for a mid-career MBA. If you have a mind that is open to new opportunities, it is always possible to use the career plateau to your advantage, to grow laterally and equip yourself for the future. Ruchira is a perfect example of someone who turned what others would call a difficulty into a novel opportunity for herself.

Networking

When I look back at my education and career, I realize that, despite being a conscientious student, I did not manage to extract full value from my course at IIMA. One of the main reasons was my own inhibition, with its roots in a conservative upbringing. Much of the learning on campuses happens outside the classroom, in informal discussions, at odd hours of the day or night. The inability to hang around with the boys means that your knowledge is limited to what the teachers teach you, more so if like me, you were from the pre-Internet era. While the Internet has greatly reduced one's dependence on fellow students or colleagues, an informal network remains a great source of information and knowledge. Sadly, even today, family responsibilities and societal norms prevent young women from taking full advantage of networking opportunities, on campuses or at work.

There was another rather comical reason why my network remained somewhat limited in the beginning of the course, one that I learnt of a few years after I left campus. As it happened, apart from being an introvert, I had also led a fairly protected life, being the daughter of a senior police officer. It was natural, therefore, that my parents decided to drop me off at the campus. At the time, one of my father's batchmates was posted as the commissioner of police (CP), Ahmedabad. The trip also turned out to be a bit of a social occasion for them. My father's first posting had been in Ahmedabad, but that was thirty years earlier, before the bifurcation of India's states on a linguistic basis. At dinner, the day before going to the campus, conversation veered to the city of Ahmedabad and the two officers realized that Vastrapur, where IIMA is located, was a distant suburb and one that my father was unaware of. In typical police fashion, the CP asked for a pilot vehicle to escort us there. While we were used to these kinds of arrangements, it was not a very common occurrence for two police cars with *laal battis* to enter an educational institute. Some senior boys were witness to this and apparently, word quickly went around that I was someone who was not to be messed around with!

On a more serious note, the networks you make with batchmates during your professional degrees are far more lasting and useful as compared to the ones you make in school or college. The alumni network is a great place to make new contacts, especially since there is great camaraderie and a sense of bonding between people from the same B-school, engineering or medical college or school of architecture. Women who marry after having worked for a few years get known professionally by their maiden names. It comes as no surprise, therefore, that as women marry late, they opt to retain their maiden names. It is just so much more convenient, and no one raises an eyebrow any more.

You will remember Arpita as the girl who made her way to IIT Kharagpur without attending a coaching class and got interview calls to all but one of the IIMs for the PGP. Arpita now works in the male-dominated oil and gas sector in a business development role.

She says, 'Once in a while when my colleagues go out for a drink in the evening, I do get invited. But many a time I can sense the discomfort when they want to crack a not-so-innocent joke and I am around. While I was on very good terms with my male friends in college, at the workplace my relationship with my boss or colleagues is mostly formal. So, crossing that boundary and cracking dirty jokes with them is a strict no-no for me, whereas for my male colleagues, it is very normal. This leads to a stronger bond among the men, whereas I am mostly left on the sidelines, being nice and cordial.'

While Arpita enjoys the trust and respect of her colleagues, she admits that this is a gender-linked handicap in her sector where women are in such a small minority.

Traditionally, men have networked over a smoke or drinks. A few decades ago, some women tried to break into this club by aping men. They tried to do this by smoking and drinking themselves as also by dressing and swearing like men. I don't know if this strategy worked at an individual level but I doubt it helped break any glass ceiling or did anything to further the cause of women. In sectors like media, advertising and journalism where the gender ratio is more balanced and people work in close proximity, women are less likely to be judged if they smoke. But in most other industries, by and large, women still feel uncomfortable smoking in public. So they end up missing out on a lot of informal interaction that often includes an exchange of not merely gossip but also valuable information about the industry, new opportunities, etc. Shweta, a young manager, sounded helpless while telling me that despite knowing the hazards of smoking, she did not give it up, just so she could remain part of the information chain! While women persevere with bumping up their representation, they must find non-conventional ways of networking at the office as well as offsites and conferences, which are essentially extended workplaces.

Sukanya Kripalu often found herself the only woman in the room at sales conferences. She says she networked with delegates and colleagues at dinner, and once she had finished meeting the people she wanted to (and before the others got more drunk!), she quietly made her way to her hotel room.

'We underplay the psychological strength in numbers. We don't always acknowledge the disadvantage we face,' says executive coach Promila Ayyangar. 'You find highly skewed gender diversity in several industries even today, especially in leadership roles. In industries like IT training, where I spent my early years, the percentage of women was much higher and that made the environment a lot more psychologically safe and conducive to building an unbiased, merit-based culture,' she adds.

Networking requires social skills and even in sectors where being under-represented is not an issue, young girls can find it intimidating. Hema Mani, as chief human resources officer (CHRO) at Lennox International, is involved with their hiring process. They mainly hire fresh graduates from engineering colleges from across the country, a significant percentage of the hires being young women. While it is wonderful to note that many of these bright women come from small towns, Hema finds them social misfits in the corporate world. In her experience, 'They are intelligent but not smart; they have been encouraged to work hard but have poor communication skills. When they meet the girls from larger cities, they find that they dress differently, have different eating habits and even watch different kinds of TV serials. Typically, young people bond over these things but here the gap is too wide. Men from smaller towns, too, face this initially, but they hang out with boys from the bigger cities after work and somehow learn fast. The girls, on the other hand, are expected to head home right after work and so don't have the same opportunities to catch up. These shortcomings become more glaring later on as social skills such as communication and networking are critical to be considered for leadership positions.'

Going to business or even social events can be daunting for anyone, but more so for young women who haven't yet made contacts in the industry and are too inhibited to walk up to strangers and introduce themselves. Taking a colleague along, at least initially, can help you feel both comfortable and confident. Once you have a couple of contacts, you can always make plans to network together and grow the group.

With diversity and inclusion gaining prominence on corporate agendas, age-old practices like going out for a drink after work are now being discouraged as they are not considered gender-neutral. Moreover, there are enough opportunities to bond with colleagues during office hours or even at office parties, picnics and conferences, and one can make the most of these by being an active participant.

Women have to achieve critical mass in the workplace. Only then will the awkwardness of a 'boys' club' monopoly over coveted roles go away.

'The same principle holds true of every minority group based on sexual orientation, education, work experience or gender,' says Abhijit Bhaduri, leadership coach. 'Achieving critical mass in the aspirational roles makes the invisible groups visible.'

While that may be true, unless the majority chooses to become inclusive, the minorities will continue to remain in ghettoes and not get access to the larger talent pool.

Acquiring a professional degree is only the start of the journey. Women tend to, in a sense, stick to the syllabus. They excel in their functional areas but stop there. Doing well at what is in the curriculum is important, but it is the extracurriculars like communication skills, personality, and the ability to influence and lead that make your CV interesting and help you get noticed. That is what investing in yourself is all about.

Making Your Presence Felt

Networking is not the only challenge for women. A bigger one perhaps is of being overlooked or not being heard in a group. Even in modern times, stereotypes exist. While interacting with women, people assume that they must be working in support functions, in softer roles like HR and communications, rather than in leadership roles or more serious functions like finance or strategy. In office set-ups, somehow jobs like organizing parties, taking notes and making coffee, fall into the laps of women; even women managers, not necessarily secretaries. There are numerous ways in which unconscious bias rears its ugly head. After all, men, too, are victims of their conditioning! Women get talked over, ignored or find themselves being talked down to. You know the behaviour is common and universal when there's a specific word that's coined to describe it. 'Mansplaining' is a term used when a man typically explains something to a woman in a condescending or patronizing manner, assuming she needs someone to explain things to her.

Can you think of a time when someone mansplained something to you or you observed it in the workplace? What was your response?

Looking the part goes a long way in making your presence felt, and you will see a number of senior women indulging in power dressing. A saree or suit adds weight to the personality. Women themselves begin to feel more mature and confident when dressed formally. Personally, I have found that taking a junior colleague along to a meeting automatically helped set the power equation right. The junior goes about setting up the presentation while I engage in conversation and setting the tone for the meeting. Subtly dropping hints about your qualifications, designation, work experience and achievements lays the ground for a proper level of conversation.

For important meetings, it is a good idea to research the person you will be meeting and look for commonalities or shared interests that would help towards creating a bond. Sites like LinkedIn are gold mines of information and you can steer the small talk to the identified topics. Prepare well for meetings. First impressions are strong and lasting and help get over most biases. There is a good chance that the other person too, would have looked you up online. A strong social media presence can help establish your credentials even before you meet. It is also far classier as compared to having to talk about your work experience or achievements yourself.

Anita Sanghi recalls one of her former managers, a non-Indian, thought one needed to be in a suit and thump aggressively on the table to be an executive . . . until he came to India. Here, he met senior women, including Anita, bold in her red bindi and saree—but soft-spoken and an incredibly effective leader. Anita's leadership style was always empathetic and gentle. Women don't need to stick to stereotypes, neither do men. The burden is not on women to be empathetic, and it is not on men to be aggressive. Leadership has been portrayed as very gendered, but Anita's message is that it shouldn't be.

I have always felt that quality scores over quantity, so if you can make a few good points firmly and with conviction, it is better than screaming at the top of your voice to be heard. After clearing the CAT written exam, I found myself the lone woman at the group discussion stage. The rest of the group consisted of engineers with work experience at one of the leading auto majors in Pune. The case was about some production problem that involved a lathe machine, and here I was, the only non-engineer who had never even seen a lathe! The guys seemed to know each other and kept reinforcing each other's points, keeping the discussion among themselves. I remember making just a couple of points based on logic and common sense, but making them calmly and confidently, well enough to get me through anyway!

Women have softer voices and when they try to speak louder or more passionately, they can sound shrill and agitated. That is one of the reasons why women are mistaken to be overemotional. Work on your voice to see how you can sound calm, yet effective. Make allies of other women or supportive male colleagues. They can help your cause if there are particularly chauvinistic colleagues who keep interrupting you. You, too, need to return the favour and support them in similar circumstances.

Most importantly, groom yourself to be confident and to stand up for yourself. From time to time, and definitely when you seem to be at the receiving end of gender-biased treatment, ask yourself what a man would have done in a similar situation. I am not suggesting at all that women should ape men blindly. After all, they are not perfect either. At the same time, they seem to handle a few things better than women do, like networking and backing themselves without being overwhelmed by self-doubt or guilt. We could learn those through observation. Be prepared at all times so that whenever you open your mouth, they know you mean business. And if it is still a struggle, know that sometimes you are bound to get hurt, so develop a thick skin. Don't give up just because someone else decided to act like an idiot.

Managing Your Finances

Sadhana and her husband are both from IIMs and are now in their mid-forties. When I broached the topic of managing money, she laughed, almost as if I had asked her a trick question. Just when I got the feeling that I had touched upon a sensitive topic, she let me in on a closely guarded secret. Sadhana was so caught up in the demands of a high-pressure job and a young child, that leaving the handling of her investments entirely to the husband she trusted seemed a huge relief. Things soured between them a few years later and Sadhana realized that she was lost as far as matters related to her investments were concerned. She asked a financial adviser friend to help her manage her portfolio, which was so far being handled by her husband. Their marriage survived but the experience left Sadhana wiser and financially more savvy.

Financial independence is the first step to empowerment, and as women professionals, we have won that battle. In fact, several of the women I spoke with in the course of writing this book said that at some stage or the other they have earned more than their husbands. Isn't it odd then that most of them are clueless about money matters and leave it to their husbands or fathers to manage their hard-earned money? Financial literacy is a life skill that one needs to acquire early in life. Even if your spouse is better placed to handle the responsibility, you need to be completely in the know about your own investments. When relationships sour, money is one of the first issues that comes up, and if you are not in charge, you might find it hard to suddenly take control.

A bright young doctor couple I met worked out a plan that they thought was most practical. She had a job while he had a thriving practice, so they figured that his income that involved a significant cash portion would be spent on household expenses. Seemed like a smart thing to do except that when the marriage started falling apart, the husband started claiming ownership of the littlest of things, saying that he had paid for them!

Educational or professional brilliance, as you would have realized by now, does not always translate into financial acumen. Financial skills are life skills and we have to learn to be fully in control of our money, tax and savings.

My friend Lavanya unfortunately learnt it the hard way. We knew each other as students. She is a lovely person, traditional and very hard-working. She married a batchmate and when he moved to Singapore, she quit her job in India and went along, not sure of what job she would find there. That is when we lost touch, only to reconnect thirty years later. It was heart-warming to find that Lavanya, despite going as a trailing spouse to an alien land, had managed to do very well professionally, having worked for some top global firms. The marriage unfortunately lasted only for a decade and a half, but by then, Lavanya's career was going strong. She was, in fact, earning more than her husband, and I suspect that was one of the reasons why the relationship went south. Alimony or childcare was out of the question since she was perfectly capable of looking after her child. What Lavanya didn't realize was that while she had earned handsomely, she had not spent smartly. As she was a more hands-on parent, she paid the fees, the maid, the rent and household expenses. The assets were all built with her husband's money, so by the time the divorce came through, she was left with neither savings nor assets.

'I was too broken to stand up for my rights,' she confided. It took her a while post the divorce, to rebuild her life as well as her bank balance.

It is a well-known fact that in many organizations the world over, there is a wage gap between genders. The explanation given is that men are better negotiators. While that may be true, and I've heard so many women say that they don't have a clue how to go about it, I suspect it has to do with self-worth as well. Women often underrate themselves.

Maliha was afraid that if she negotiated hard while interviewing for a job she desperately wanted, she would be rejected. She shared her fear with her husband who assured her that it was perfectly normal to negotiate and, in fact, encouraged her not to hold back. Maliha, with her new-found confidence, ended up getting both, her dream job as well as a great package.

Not everyone is as lucky as Maliha to get the right advice. Before Tejasvi Ravi became a healthcare investor, she used to be chief of staff at Medanta Hospitals and handled a large number of job applications. In her experience, men writing in for jobs typically ask for a 30 per cent raise but women agree to come in at the previous salary or even take cuts. Interestingly, Tejasvi admits to committing the same crime herself! Looking back, she realizes that the lack of aggression can be viewed as a lack of desire or ambition. On the other hand, any form of aggression gets a woman branded as a 'difficult' woman that no one wants to work with. Some women ascribe the reluctance to negotiate to a woman's fear that acting tough during the interview could potentially diminish her chances of getting a concession, should she require flexibility in working hours, a change in role, etc. Like many other things in her life, this is a tough balancing act.

Deepali Naair was fortunate to get not only support but also professional advice from her husband, a senior HR professional. He told her exactly how the negotiation would go and what she needed to do. When you have learnt the finer points of the art of negotiation and also have the confidence to handle it, the result can only be a happy one. The important thing is understanding which skills are useful and then investing time and energy learning them.

I have observed that when women, even professional women meet, they hardly ever discuss work, salaries, opportunities, negotiations, etc. This is probably because, as I mentioned earlier, women, unlike men, don't define themselves by their careers. Their lives involve simultaneous conversations with the domestic help, relatives, class teachers, neighbours and, of course, clients and colleagues. Many of their friends are homemakers. So 'What do you do?' is a potentially awkward question. Homemakers sound guilty saying they are 'only housewives' when in reality managing a home is, in many ways, more challenging than running an office.

A man's identity, on the other hand, is almost entirely centred on his work. When men meet, they start talking shop; if not right away, then definitely once they are done discussing sport. They are better informed and better networked, and that is something we can learn from them. So, while women pride themselves in having more interesting conversations that straddle a wide range of topics from films and books to food and fashion, we would do ourselves a favour by being more clued in about our professional interests.

Getting Ready to Be a Leader

I dislike the term 'women leaders'. I think there are only two categories of leaders or founders—good leaders and bad leaders, and that has absolutely nothing to do with gender. The way both genders are wired and conditioned does create certain strengths and weaknesses, but they are not things that define leaders.

When organizations consider candidates for leadership positions, they generally consider three things—the functional expertise of the managers, their team management skills and their leadership capability. A number of research studies show that women generally score high on functional skills. They are often better than men when it comes to things like attention to detail. In fact, at times, attention to detail, which has all along been a strength, gradually starts coming in the way. This is because, as leaders, you need to delegate and, therefore, learn to let go. Leadership is not only about your own performance but your ability to get the best out of your team. Good leaders, you will find, resist micromanaging their team, preferring instead to trust the capabilities of their subordinates. A cliché that comes to mind, an apt one nevertheless, is: 'What brought you thus far is not what is going to take you forward.' Letting go, therefore, is an essential skill and one that is not as easy as it sounds.

Sometimes, leadership roles come up unexpectedly or under adverse circumstances and the requirement is to find a capable leader to take charge of the team, even if she/he comes from a somewhat different functional area. It could be a wonderful career opportunity for a leader to broaden her experience. However, it also involves a high degree of learning in a short period of time to get to some level of subject matter expertise in the new role. It is then quite likely that you don't have the answers to all the questions that might come your way. Interestingly, it has been observed that in such a situation, men find it easier to say, 'I will come back to you on this,' whereas women feel inadequate if they can't provide the answer to every question, there and then. I won't be surprised if this in some way is related to the imposter syndrome or the fact that women tend to constantly underrate themselves. We must remember that leaders too, like other people, learn every day, and in a complex and uncertain environment, such situations are more likely to occur. So, one has to learn to be comfortable with it.

Anjali Mohanty was a veteran in retail banking when she was unexpectedly offered a role in corporate banking. The CEO said that the *energy* that she brought to her current role was what he thought made her suitable for the new role being offered to her.

'You need to know why you are being offered the role. You cannot be suspicious of the organization's intent. I was both surprised and thrilled by the offer and went into it with an open mind,' she says. It was a lot of hard work and learning but turned out to be the opportunity of a lifetime for her.

Madhabi Puri Buch had a similar experience when she joined SEBI, being the first professional from the private sector to be one of its full-time members on the board. While she was on home ground as far as capital markets were concerned, the regulatory nature of the job was totally new for her, and she had to hit the ground running. She says that it helped tremendously that the culture that the chairman had set was one of learning and sharing. Not only did no one raise an eyebrow when she would bluntly declare that she 'did not get it', but there was 360-degree support to explain to her how things worked. Organizational culture starts at the top and it helps hugely to have leaders with a learning mindset.

When I used to be in advertising two decades ago, several formidable women headed the media departments of leading agencies. But till recently, Nandini Dias (who has now stepped down) was the only woman heading a large media set-up. When she was appointed CEO at Lodestar Media, Nandini soon realized that her core competence—developing media strategy and innovating solutions for marketing challenges, where she'd earned most of her accolades—would not be enough. She would have to quickly develop new skills and take a few giant leaps in new areas. She needed to better understand the company's business aspects, the nuanced details of exhaustive financial statements and learn to connect the dots across multiple developments within and outside the organization.

For instance, she had a lot of friends and connections but seldom needed to nurture these bonds for the purpose of business. She would have to cultivate new relationships, which would now become critical to the operations. This quick recognition of the need to step up and promptly upgrade each of these aspects is what set her on her way. She also realized that she now personally represented the brand more than ever and would have to invest more effort in meeting people and building relationships. This was something she confesses was clearly out of her instinctive comfort zone.

Business networking is not only about knowing people but about gaining from conversations with people from your circle. It could mean closing business deals or exploring joint opportunities. Like Nandini, Falguni Nayar, too, admits that it was a skill she had to learn with some degree of effort. Falguni says that initially, while she did go along with her husband Sanjay, who is a great networker, she was shy to talk about business-related topics and stuck to social small talk. It was only after about fifteen years of working, when she attended some leadership sessions conducted by McKinsey, that she realized the importance of business networking. The higher you climb on the corporate ladder, the bigger and more varied the challenges. So, an early understanding of what it takes can help prepare you for the role better. Attending conferences, having discussions with other business associates or attending professional development courses are all wonderful ways to invest early in your career.

The second aspect of a leader's job involves managing a team. Years of conditioning have ensured that women are great at understanding and getting along with people with different temperaments and in all kinds of situations. Consequently, it makes most women perfect candidates to lead teams, unless of course, we shoot ourselves in the foot by giving up what we have in trying to be like men!

The nurturing side to their personality makes women more inclined to reconciliation and peacemaking, and consequently not very comfortable in confrontational situations at work. However, as leaders, you would routinely need to give feedback, which may not always be favourable, or even fire people who are poor performers or have integrity issues. Such situations are always awkward and unpleasant but need to be handled firmly and promptly.

A very important lesson I learnt fairly early in life was from watching a senior in my advertising agency handle team meetings. Whenever a new campaign was presented to him, he would begin by listing all the aspects that he liked and he thought worked for the brand. Then slowly and pleasantly, he would get to all the things that he thought needed to be relooked at. Often, the list of negatives was longer and more significant compared to the list of positives, yet the systematic demolition of the campaign was done gently and tactfully. I realized that, whereas my first instinct would have been to bluntly tell the team that the campaign was not working and that they would have to go back to the drawing board, he delivered the same message without demoralizing the team. They might have got it wrong on that particular day but still had to stay motivated to come back with a better idea the following day. 'Zor ka jhatka dheere se lage' (a rude shock that is delivered gently) works beautifully in this part of the world. Luckily, I was young and absorbed the lesson quickly.

Great communication skills can be an asset to any leader. One doesn't need to be an extrovert or a flamboyant speaker, but to be effective, you must be able to communicate with credibility and conviction. An inspiring leader is invariably a good communicator, and it takes years to hone the skill. Presentations, talks, interviews must be rich in content but when delivered with flair, can be even more memorable and inspiring. One has to grab every opportunity to address groups or speak in public starting from the early years, so that by the time you become a leader, you have mastered the art and gained the confidence.

Roopa Kudva believes that a key skill of leadership involves managing stakeholders. You have to deal with the government, policymakers, board members, investors and other such entities. Organizations are sometimes unsure of whether a woman leader would be up for the challenge. Will she be too soft and someone who can be pushed over? There are already a few women in India and across the world who are showing us that women can be equally fearless, outspoken and tough. More women in key positions will help break this misconception of women being meek pushovers.

Sunita Venkatraman has worked as global head of insights and analytics and has observed both male and female leaders in India, Singapore and the US closely. Men are comfortable with other men as they bond over sport and typical male humour, she feels. It is more a case of self-selection rather than discrimination against women. Through this, the leadership model only gets further reinforced as being stereotypically male. Sunita also believes that leadership involves some amount of politics and subtle manipulation where every leader forms his/her groupies or supporters.

'A lot of women feel disadvantaged when it comes to such behaviour. Not everyone has the stomach for the politics that senior leadership involves,' she feels.

Leadership roles come with a lot of pressure and leaders might be subject to criticism. They, therefore, need to be shrewd and learn to take the brickbats along with the bouquets. A life of pressure and responsibility comes with its share of long hours and travel, and requires the leader to be energetic and mentally alert. An exercise routine and a healthy lifestyle are habits worth cultivating from a young age, as well as investments that can yield rich dividends at a later age. These days you will find most leaders also make time for a hobby like sport, music or photography. These are great ways to de-stress and can add an interesting dimension to the leader's personality. It goes without saying that leaders need to have their priorities clear and also be great time managers to fit all this in their already busy schedules.

1) In your line of work, what are the skills that can take you ahead? What are you doing to get better at them?
2) How comfortable and clued in are you when it comes to handling your finances?

What Makes a Powerful Personal Brand?

- Mastery in your area of work—Being someone who can be trusted to deliver on any task or whose opinion can be relied upon and sought, if there is an issue.
- Uniqueness in what you bring to the table—Having a skill set and experience that makes you unique and therefore not easily replaceable. Staying relevant over time.
- Visibility—Being known for your work and having connections and relationships that are useful when information or help is sought.
- Communication skills—Having the ability to influence, convince, persuade and motivate through the spoken and written word.
- Personal appearance and grooming—Coming through as someone who is professional and well mannered.
- Confidence and energy level—Having the capacity to actively engage and focus for long hours. Displaying enthusiasm and optimism even in pressure situations.
- Wow factor—Extracurricular aspects like hobbies and other interests. A hook, beyond work, that people remember you for.

Chapter 4

Tripping on Guilt

One of the most common questions that plagues young professional women is, 'Can women have it all?' I suspect the question has its roots in the changing definition of what today's women want from their lives. Over the years, the prevalent notion in society has been that women can either be good mothers or good professionals. The construct suggests an *either/or* situation, not an *and* one. If a woman is successful at work, the assumption is that she couldn't have made time for her home and family; she must be a poor homemaker and an uncaring mother. This explains why super successful women are not automatic choices as great role models. Similarly, a homemaker is assumed to be more devoted to her family, which is why, when a woman quits a job and decides to stay at home, it is seen as a selfless act. There is this constant inner struggle within women to understand their idea of success and then figure out their priorities. They, too, can fall prey to the thinking that if you find success in one aspect of your life, you might have missed out on the rest. This fear of missing out or FOMO, as it is now called, is why guilt is a constant companion for the female species. Earlier, FOMO was about missing your baby's first steps, not being able to attend PTA meetings or spending less time with your ageing parents. As women are making rapid strides up the corporate ladder, FOMO about missing promotions or plum postings also got added on. Life only got more complicated!

Women have always been known to be master jugglers. They can be the most resourceful and imaginative multitaskers. Men don't even qualify in this particular race. I have often marvelled at myself for the wide variety of tasks that sit side by side on my to-do list. They could involve presentations at high-profile events, buying groceries, coordinating a job with the carpenter or recording a song for some friend's Zoom party. And yet there are times when doing all you can just isn't enough and you are left with a feeling that every woman is familiar with—GUILT.

As I mentioned earlier, our multitasking skills need to be at their peak around the age of thirty-five when career pressures (both your own as well as those of your spouse) typically collide with the presence or planning of children. As Indra Nooyi puts it, 'For women, the biological clock and the career clock are totally in conflict with each other.' The first ten years of your working life tend to be the most challenging and, therefore, the most guilt-ridden, but once you have crossed that initial hurdle, it becomes far more manageable, and careers are far less likely to trip.

My own story as a thirty-five-year-old involves a school play that my seven-year-old took part in. Every year, various classes put up popular plays and my son, being musically inclined, often got a singer's role, especially when a musical was being staged. I remember being particularly thrilled that year when, for a change, he got a plum acting role. He was to be the Wicked Witch of the West in *The Wizard of Oz* and I spent a lot of time and money getting the costume organized. Rehearsals went on for days and when the little fellow returned from school, I would get a complete rundown of what happened at practice. When the kids were young, I made it a point to wrap up work by the time they returned from school, so I was pretty updated on what was happening in their lives. Two days before the show, there was a dress rehearsal and so I made my way to the school auditorium carrying the costume that I had so proudly put together.

'Oh, you are finally here,' said the dramatics teacher, on seeing me. 'I almost gave the part to someone else, thinking you were not interested.' I was shocked. The teacher was a working woman too, and yet she expected another working woman to just hang around during rehearsals like some of the other mothers, who had more time on their hands. I couldn't believe I was being made out to be the selfish, uncaring working mother!

So, for all your hard work, some days you might falter or be made to feel guilty. Luckily, such days are few and far between and even more importantly, you will survive them to tell your story. The details of the incident, truth be told, have blurred with the years. I have long forgotten the name of the teacher. What remains, however, is a lovely picture of the wicked witch who actually looked rather sweet!

* * *

Guilt is an integral part of a woman's psyche and manifests itself more acutely in working professional women. The origin of guilt, I suspect, lies in women's desire to please everyone around them, as also their sense of failure when they can't perform a task to their own satisfaction. As urban working women multitask more than other women and take on considerably more responsibilities, they find many more reasons to feel guilty. Add to that the pressure of having to miss out on family events or looking your best at your friend's wedding and we have a perfect recipe for a nervous wreck. Not reaching out to a friend in need, forgetting to call your mother as promised, an accidental fall by the toddler, missing out on some items in your self-created, impossible job list . . . the reasons can be endless. Seemingly all minor, these reasons can have a cumulative ability to overwhelm and even cause women to opt out of careers. Studies throw up the most common tripping points in women's careers. Avtar's annual research, Viewport 2019, reveals that motherhood challenges (45 per cent) and maternity (35 per cent) are the most common reasons for women to take a break from their careers. At 16 per cent, elder care responsibility is another critical reason.

Marriage—The First Tripping Point

Increasingly, young professionals are realizing that the first potential tripping point is marriage and are putting it off for as long as possible, even sometimes questioning the need to get married. Parents are initially uncomfortable and awkward with a daughter who chooses to focus on her career rather than get married and get increasingly worried and anxious as she grows older. Society makes parents feel as if they fell short on efforts in finding a match for her and they, in turn, pass on the guilt to the girl.

Marriage adds two new dimensions to a woman's life—the responsibility of running a home and the desire to please the new in-laws. In a joint family, if the family has employed a cook, the responsibility may be partial and life may be easier. But if the mother-in-law is hands-on with everything, then she is likely to expect an intern who meets her exacting standards. Working late, travel, offsites, training programmes—anything that upsets her normal working hours can be a huge source of stress and guilt for the new daughter-in-law. Pleasantly forewarning the family of such possibilities and taking on other responsibilities at home can help set more realistic expectations and preserve relationships. Young couples now prefer to live independently, if they can afford it, but that involves trying out various combinations of domestic help, cooks and tiffin services, especially if the couple works odd and long hours or the jobs involve outstation travel. Eating out and ordering in, they quickly discover, can be equally disastrous on the waist as it is on the wallet. The bulk of the responsibility of managing the home and kitchen inevitably falls on the woman. As the joke goes, when women take their marriage vows and say 'I do', they don't realize that it will be that way for the rest of their lives! Even in today's age, especially in India, you need a lot of luck to find a man who is capable of running a home and willing to do it even after marriage.

Chitra Ranade is one such lucky lady. Her husband, Chinmay, who is an equally successful senior manager, is also a competent cook. They both have demanding jobs that often involve working late hours. They are a perfect DINK (Double Income, No Kids) couple who have resisted hiring a cook so far and prefer to eat simple, home-made meals as far as possible. The days Chitra works late and Chinmay doesn't, she comes home to a hot meal and a husband who understands her compulsions at work. She is spared the guilt of both working late and keeping the husband hungry.

Helping the wife stay free from guilt and stress is without a doubt the greatest gift a husband can give her.

The Maternity Break and How to Manage It

There is absolutely no doubt that a maternity break is the single most challenging stage in a woman's career. A pregnancy is typically announced and celebrated in society as 'good news'. It is the time when women are pampered and looked after. For working women, however, it could well mean that your teams and organizations see you as physically and emotionally vulnerable, compromised in terms of productivity, and incapacitated when it comes to high-pressure projects or travel.

As a senior HR head told me, in order to counter this, many women try very hard to be active and work right till they go into labour, just to prove that pregnancy doesn't mean you are out of action. They want to swing back into the thick of things right after their delivery, in line with the highly controversial recommendation of Marissa Mayer, the former CEO of Yahoo. You might have read about how she went to work after just two weeks of delivering a baby. The HR head made it clear that the company did nothing to pressurize its employees to return early and that it was every woman's individual choice how late into her pregnancy she wanted to work. My personal view has been that becoming a parent is a huge responsibility and the early days and months are important, involving not only breastfeeding but also seeing the baby through immunization and teething and other such important milestones. It is a trying as well as an emotional period for a young mother, and unless she has a dependable and caring support system in the form of a mother, mother-in-law or trained maid, it is very difficult to separate her from her baby. I feel that taking six months off to look after your baby does not make much difference to a career that spans over thirty-five to forty years but can pay huge dividends to both the mother and child.

Now, of course, in India, women are entitled to six months of paid maternity leave (which is an issue that is being debated and we will tackle that in later chapters), with an option to extend it without pay, giving the new mother a little more time to settle the baby down. Even then, when it is time to go back to work, women struggle with what is effectively the cutting of the umbilical cord for the second time. With such an attractive and emotionally engaging distraction at home now, the return to work needs to be both smooth and fulfilling. The onus of this falls on both the young woman as well as the organization.

'The key thing is for women to see the break as a temporary thing,' suggests Natasha Ramarathnam, an IIMA alumna from Hyderabad, whose own maternity break extended longer than expected as she lives in a nuclear family and found it difficult to manage career and home. If the maternity leave extends for too long, staying at home can become comfortable and careers can easily get derailed. Natasha also feels that when women are at home on a maternity break, they find that more than their share of domestic chores starts falling in their laps.

'You are at home anyway so can you supervise the plumber and also get the water filter changed?' would be a familiar narrative.

Natasha warns young mothers that this is an irreversible process and you will continue doing all the work that the spouse did before your break, even after you join back. As it is, women take on more than their fair share of domestic chores. Others, too, say that during the maternity break, you should deviate from your routine as little as possible so that the transition back to work is smoother. Once the baby settles down to a schedule, the new mother should try to get back to her normal eating and sleeping schedule, with some me time thrown in as well.

An interesting fallout of the Covid-19 pandemic and the resultant lockdown has been that with limited or no access to domestic help, men and young adults have had to do their share of household chores. It has been a fabulous learning experience, particularly for the well-to-do, and my hope is that they continue the good work long after the virus has been conquered!

Managing the maternity break well is critical and, depending on their situation and support systems, women resort to different strategies.

Dhanashree Shirodkar Joglekar comes from a family of working women and has worked in several top finance firms. She is a proud mother of two little girls. She is full of tips for young working mothers, things which she believes you need to plan well in advance, before the baby is born, so that you have childcare options ready and don't have to rush when the actual need arises. Get a list of nannies or day-care centres close to home, and talk to mothers in your area to get feedback about these places. Finding a proper nanny or day care and settling your child in takes at least two to three months, she feels.

'If there are many issues with the childcare system in the initial days, then a mother's confidence is shaken to the core. She feels worthless and constantly questions her ability to be a good mother,' she warns.

Amita Parekh is a partner at Boston Consulting Group (BCG). When she had her son, she used to be a consultant and her job involved considerable travel. Being part of a joint family, Amita had wonderful family support when it came to childcare. Even with all the support though, one needs to prepare oneself to rejoin, she feels.

'Although I had an option to work from home for the first few months when I was doing an internal project, I made it a point to go to office and wave him bye so that he knows Mom is gone. I feel as kids get older, it becomes tougher for them to accept the fact that the mother has left.'

She recommends starting slowly and then ramping up, making the transition easy for the baby as well as the mother.

'I started slow, so for the first six months I did internal projects, then worked part-time at 60 per cent, increased it to 80 per cent and as the kid just started nursery, planned to be back to 100 per cent. What this helped me do is slowly and steadily make the kid and myself used to the fact that Mom has long hours and cannot be part of every single event in his life. For the first fifteen to eighteen months, while he was still being breastfed, I did not travel overnight, then slowly started with select domestic trips and then did a few short international trips as well.'

'Whether it is a house help or a day care, you need someone whom you completely trust, have personally observed closely and verified for all legal purposes. Spend at least a month before joining back, to observe if your child is comfortable and happy with the arrangement. It's a good idea to instal a home camera or check with the day care for the same, just to be extra cautious,' suggests Shweta Agarwal, an engineer–MBA who has recently turned entrepreneur. When the mother returns to work, she should be guilt-free and her mind must be at peace in the knowledge that her baby is in safe hands.

For people like me who barely got a month and a half as maternity leave, the idea of six months' paid leave seems like a real perk. The option of an extended but unpaid break was always available to women earlier, but looking back, I suspect that since the rejoining date was open-ended, organizations rarely planned your career post the break. Now, as Dhanashree, Amita and Shweta pointed out, the new mothers and their organizations are better placed to plan the 'after' life. It came as a surprise to me that there are many women who don't want to exercise their right to the six months' leave. The fear of missing out is so high that they opt to go back to work earlier. It now seems obvious that when men are wary of taking even three weeks of paternity leave, women too, particularly in highly competitive careers like investment banking or management consultancy, feel that they will get left behind if they are out of action for six months. It is interesting that women in earlier generations only feared missing out on seeing their children grow up, but today's woman experiences FOMO both at home and at work!

Six months is a long time, and in today's fast-paced world, there is a good chance that teams, organizations and indeed the business itself will have moved on by the time you get back. While maternity leave is meant to be a time for the mother and child to bond, it is equally important that, after the initial few weeks of rest and recuperation, you start making some time for yourself. Use this time to keep yourself abreast of what is happening at work. Technology has made it very easy to stay in touch with colleagues. An informal network like WhatsApp helps you stay updated on projects, people and even gossip. You might be scornful of something like gossip but continuing to be part of the office grapevine helps you get back into the network easily. People who return after a longish gap, even to their old organizations, can start feeling like outsiders if they are not familiar with what is going on. It is possible that you might have moved to your parents' or in-laws' house for the delivery and they may not have a high-speed Internet connection or gadgets that you might be used to. Even if it comes at a cost, prepare and make sure that you have all that you need to stay in touch.

Having a more formal network like email with your teammates and getting a weekly snapshot of the goings-on in the business helps immensely. It ensures that when you rejoin, you don't go in totally clueless. The important thing is to not be totally cut off from your work. Hema Mani thinks that if organizations onboard employees who come back from a long break, it will go a long way in resettling them at work.

Encourage your husband to avail of his paternity leave while you return to work. If maternity and paternity leave are staggered smartly, it will give the baby more time under the care of at least one parent. Of course, that will mean that the husband must feel confident about looking after the baby independently. Remember that it is almost certain that you will be better than your husband at handling the baby, but unless you allow him to make mistakes and improve, he never will. I know of many fathers who take excellent care of their babies, and we must encourage men to be hands-on fathers, not stand-in babysitters to their own kids. There is absolutely no reason for a mother to feel either embarrassed or guilty about that.

Getting back to the rhythm of work can take a bit of time and the anxiety of leaving a baby behind at home doesn't leave a mother easily. There will always be days when the little one looks unwell or you have been awake the entire night. From time to time, the support system might even look shaky. All this can hinder your performance at work. There will be insensitive people who will make you feel guilty or selfish or even inadequate. A common complaint seems to be that a woman who takes the day off to tend to a sick child is labelled unprofessional, while a father who does the same is hailed as being devoted. As I mentioned earlier, a large part of society still believes that men work to support their families whereas women work for themselves. That warped view is something that we need to live with (and work to change), at least for the present. You need to be resilient and thick-skinned at such times, as these are typical situations in which women are tempted to throw in the towel. It is sad when a situation at home, which could well be temporary and not really serious, costs a professional her entire career.

Very often, when women return to their organizations after a maternity break, they get a feeling that everything has changed in their absence. Their old teams could be working on new projects, and they themselves could be assigned new roles or become part of new teams. Generally, work and colleagues have moved on while they were away and their old workplace, which was their comfort zone, now seems unfamiliar. As a new mother, you might find this a bit too much to handle, especially since you are not at your productive best. It is likely that you might have to report to someone who was at the same level as you or even a junior who got promoted in the meantime. If you start feeling that you have lost out at work as well, remind yourself that there will always be opportunities to catch up if you show patience and positivity and are determined to do well. There will be phases in life, once the children need less attention, when the focus can shift back to your career and you will be ready to take up the most challenging assignments. To give you an analogy from cricket, even the best batsmen wait for the opportune moment to hit sixes and fours. Till then, enjoy the quiet ones and twos that keep the score moving and you will find that in the end you have managed to rack up a big total.

Being with a good employer is, without doubt, a very important factor in ensuring that you don't slip in your career. Changing jobs around the time you plan to have children is definitely not advisable as you might not have built equity yet with the new employer. If your leave extends beyond what the employer's policies allow and you need to look for a job after a three to four-year break, that could be a challenge as well since recruiters look for the most recent experience while hiring. I am told law firms are reluctant to take back people who have taken a break. So while *The Good Wife* made wonderful viewing, we clearly don't have too many Alicia Florricks in real life!

If your break is likely to be longer and you cannot get back to your old job, do something related to your line of work till you get back. Invest in courses, learn new skills or do projects that will not make your break look like a hole in your CV. I am told that in Bengaluru, there are groups of women from the IT sector who are mothers with young children and who meet frequently for what might be considered as learning-cum-networking sessions. I think it is a great way to bond with a group with whom you have much in common, both personally and professionally. They discuss what they have read, maybe watch videos together, explore opportunities to get back to work and, of course, also indulge in regular mommy talk. Taking up a new job after a long break could even involve a pay cut, so be ready for it. A slow start is better than no start, and there is a good chance that you will get back on track pretty soon. The trick, as I said before, is to keep yourself up to date even while you are away and keep doing or studying something relevant to your sphere of work. Bringing a unique set of skills to the table always makes the candidate look more attractive.

Am I a Good Enough Mother?

For mothers, the term that evokes guilt at its highest level is 'latchkey children'. The imagery of young kids being lonely and unsupervised at home, even for a short while, makes women freak out. Devyani, a consultant working in London, would go to work, leaving her four-year-old with a maid at home. The child knew that the mother would return at 5 p.m. but was not old enough to read the time. So every day around 4 p.m., she would start asking the maid if it was five o'clock. The child would ask the same question every couple of minutes and sometimes it would get a bit too much for the maid to handle. So, to avoid answering the girl, she would hide from her. Not having either the mother or the maid around would make the child howl loudly. On one occasion, the little one asked the maid to telephone Devyani at work. Devyani told the child that she was leaving but realized since she took the subway, it would be a while before she got home. Her fear was that her daughter would panic and step out of the house, on to the road, to wait for her mother to return. Knowing that the underground always has a poor phone signal, the young mother got a colleague to telephone her home and keep the child calm by constantly talking to her, till she reached home. Such situations are as traumatic for mothers as they are for kids, and the imagery of what could have happened is far more horrible than the relatively harmless episode itself. When things settle down, everyone realizes that such incidents are infrequent and eventually kids (and their young mothers) grow up as well!

'The idea that your child should not grow up lonely and must have a companion at home makes most women opt for two children, but having a single child makes more sense from the career point of view,' says Gauri Chaudhari, an author and independent healthcare management consultant. A single maternity break is manageable but two breaks can set a woman's career so far back that a comeback is difficult.

Equally interesting is the question of whether to have kids early or later in your career. Both come with pros and cons and you need to figure out what works for you. The earlier you have kids, the less you have at stake. The salary is lower and so the opportunity to make up for any kind of setback even if you decide to take a slightly longer maternity break is much better. Besides, with age on your side, medical complications are likely to be fewer. However, if the husband too is young and junior, hiring good-quality help can be quite a stretch financially, and if the couple's parents are still working and maybe in another city, that option too might not be available over a longer period of time.

Madhabi Puri Buch discovered an unexpected advantage in getting married early and having her only child early as well.

'The advantage in having a child early is that by the time you are in mid-management and aspiring to get into senior management, the children are already grown up and don't require that much attention. It leaves you freer to work long hours, travel at short notice, and take on more and more challenging assignments. That can be a huge consideration, especially if you are a woman. As the pyramid gets narrower, having a child who is still young creates many more challenges that can be tough to overcome.'

In contrast, a later pregnancy can mean that you are financially more sound, with access to better care. The career, too, might be on a more solid foundation. But the spouse could be in middle management and busier and, therefore, less likely to be hands-on with the child. A late pregnancy could mean greater risk and maybe lower energy. Besides, since the position at work is likely to be a senior one, it is less likely to be left vacant till you return. On the plus side, your parents, if retired by then, might be free to step in should that be necessary. Typically, it has been observed that couples who have kids when they are older have more money and, therefore, run the risk of pampering the child excessively.

I can clearly see the trend shifting to having children late, especially since women are also marrying late. Most women I interviewed from the thirty to thirty-five-year age group were still contemplating having children. Not having children at all seems a convenient, even acceptable option, one that they might even be okay with. Parents, too, are sceptical and wonder if the hectic lifestyle of DINKs leaves any place for a child. However, it is a huge decision, and while it looks attractive and practical in the thirties, as people start crossing the age of forty, you start missing having children. In the forties and fifties, people normally start shifting their ambition from themselves to their children. Having plenty of money and no one besides yourself to spend it on can also be a major regret for DINKs. Besides, forfeiting motherhood in favour of your career is not a guilt-free choice either as our society labels such women unfeminine and selfish.

Women who are doing well at work are naturally tempted to delay motherhood till as late as possible. While it seems like the logical thing to do, going against your own biological clock comes with its own stresses and risks. Science is making great strides in helping older women conceive, but it is not always a cakewalk.

No wonder then that adoption seems like a practical option. Adoption on humanitarian grounds is definitely noble and I find many youngsters saying that when there are so many babies up for adoption, why bring another one into this world? I have many friends who have adopted children and can see how wonderful it has been for both the parents and the children. However, media coverage makes adoption sound like pre-ordering a baby without going through labour! Adoption comes with its own risks and challenges, not to mention the long-drawn-out procedure and paperwork, and in my view, must be considered as a well-thought-through choice and not an easier option.

Freezing eggs and surrogacy too are options that many articles in the media seem to put forth as a solution for career women who want to have the best of both career and family. While the technology offers hope to many mothers who might not otherwise have a chance at motherhood, having given birth and raised two children born five years apart, I can tell you with confidence that the energy required in bringing up children is far more significant than the actual nine months of pregnancy. And in five years, you will notice yourself how the energy levels have gone down. Pregnancy is visible, so everyone is in a mood to pamper and empathize with the to-be mother. Once the kids are born, life changes forever in many invisible ways.

Having grandparents or maids look after kids, while being a less stressful option, still leaves women with the feeling that they are not hands-on mothers and a fear that the kids are likely to grow closer to the 'other woman'. Management consultant Gauri Chaudhari shares interesting advice that a senior lady gave her at a time her mother-in-law offered to look after her children: 'When you have handed over your child to her, consider it as hers,' she was told. Gauri believes that it is good advice and helps prevent friction. There is no reason to doubt the mother-in-law's capabilities either. After all, she brought up your husband!

Children require time and attention till they are well into their teen years and the need to switch between children's activities and work can take its toll on the mother. Sometimes it becomes obvious enough for others to notice. I was doing very well in advertising but worked part-time while my sons were still young. My husband is in a profession that requires him to travel extensively, for several weeks at a stretch. A well-meaning senior at work suggested that I send my children to boarding school. Perfectly practical advice if you look at it, but I was not comfortable with it and continued working part-time.

I look back at my days in advertising with a great deal of fondness, but as a young mother then, I also remember the time spent just waiting for internal or client meetings. While the agency did its best to respect my timings of 11 a.m. to 4 p.m., the business by its very nature involves a number of people and departments that make long hours inevitable. For a mother waiting to get back to a young child at home, the hours definitely felt endless!

At the same time, I felt guilty every time I had to refuse travel or express my inability to attend an offsite or a training programme. Though the agency was very nice and understanding and nobody said a word, I felt terribly embarrassed. The fact that the children were being well-cared-for while we were making several successful pitches at work was not always sufficient to quieten the guilt of not being present 100 per cent at either place all the time. This feeling of constantly being torn between work and home is a common one, especially if you are committed, but the good news is that most women, including me, agree that this guilt goes down steadily over the years. So do not succumb to it!

Another advertising professional, who also chose to become an independent consultant and has even written a book recently, talked me through the dilemma she went through. She used to work full-time, comfortable in the knowledge that her two children were being looked after by her in-laws, ably assisted by a nanny. It seemed like a perfect arrangement, with loving grandparents who the kids adored, along with a good nanny who ensured that the grandparents were not overworked. As the children started growing up, my friend found that the younger child started having issues with schoolwork. The grades started dropping and the school even hinted that the child might be a slow learner. The mother's first instinct was to quit her job and focus on the child. As she addressed the academic issue, she realized that while the children were well fed and loved by the grandparents, all they did when they got back from school was to watch cookery shows that the grandmother was hooked on. It was okay when they were toddlers but not when homework started increasing. Once things got under control, the child's grades improved and the mother went back to working part-time. The boy, now a young man, got admission to an Ivy League college (and also became a good cook, thanks to all the shows he had watched with Grandma!) but has never forgotten his mother's contribution to his success.

So, while it seems tough to have it all at one time or all the time, you can have it all over your entire life, enjoying different things in different phases of your life. Unless you have exceptional support at home, you will not be at your professional best as a new mother or as you get closer to retirement. Your best years at work would be before the kids arrive and when your children are out of school and you are still young. There are peaks and plateaus in every career and they must both be seen as opportunities. The peaks are the times around which you accept new challenges and breathe easy when it comes to home and kids. The plateaus could be because you have chosen to lie low at work while family comes first. Enjoy those as well and use that phase to plan the next step.

Giving 100 per cent at work often means that you have less time for the home and the kids. It is understood that you can't drop your children to classes, attend drama rehearsals or pack surprise treats in your husband's lunch box. It could also be that your kids are under the care of your mother or mother-in-law or a maid. Children get attached to whoever they spend time with, so don't fall into the trap of competing for their love with their caregivers. While it is common for grandparents to look after grandchildren, I don't know any woman who doesn't have issues with the arrangement.

Children can make mothers feel guilty about working late, not visiting school often enough or even not throwing better birthday parties than their friends. Every mother I have spoken with has wondered, at some time or the other, if she has been a good mother or not. I suspect the role of a mother comes with far more responsibility and emotion as compared to that of a wife or daughter. Tell your children what your work means to you, how important it is, how hard you have worked to get to this position and they will respect you. Make them a part of your life and dreams just as you are a part of theirs.

While guilt is universal and seems inevitable, it is a completely useless and unproductive emotion. Those who manage it well, hang in and continue in their work life, at times with some compromise. Those who succumb to guilt, give up on their careers.

Other Tripping Points

While motherhood remains the single largest reason for women to give up their careers, there are other reasons as well. A decade ago, it was also common for women to take voluntary retirement around the time children got to the Standard XII stage. A leave requirement that is probably unique to Indian women is study leave, not for your own studies but when your children appear for their Standard X or XII board exams! Now, to prevent such leaks in the pipeline and to accommodate emergency family requirements of employees, some companies have begun to allow high-performing individuals leave to look after aged parents or a family member who is ill, etc. Most companies don't have hard-coded policies regarding such issues but you always hear of exceptions made by good bosses and good companies to deserving employees. Having a woman boss or a male boss with a working wife is considered a blessing because they understand your pressures and can be expected to be more supportive, but I guess that is not something you can have much control over!

Madhabi Puri Buch remembers a case from many years ago, of a high performer from her team who requested long leave to attend to some pressing personal matters. The team member in question had worked with the bank for close to twenty years and had consistently delivered results. Despite there being no such precedent at that time, a work from home option was worked out. Madhabi says she could get HR to agree since the person in question was a high performer and a trusted long-serving employee. The arrangement worked out beautifully and the bank had absolutely no cause for complaint. 'Job hoppers would find it difficult to create such equity in the system,' cautions Madhabi. Now, of course, hardly anyone stays with an organization for that long but commitment and top performance can help create equity even in much shorter spans.

Whatever your choice, you will always have people questioning it, criticizing it and making you feel guilty. As Amy Westervelt says about working moms in her book *Forget 'Having It All'*, 'We expect women to work like they don't have children and raise children as if they don't work.'

Letting go of your ambition and settling for something that is way below what you think you deserve can help achieve better equilibrium but comes with its own brand of guilt. A corporate life is a bigger rat race than being self-employed. Even twenty to thirty years into your career, comparisons with batchmates continue and batch parity still haunts you. I know a woman whose career was compromised somewhere along the way. She was so embarrassed when she went for batch reunions that she had printed fancy visiting cards and when batchmates asked her what she was doing, she spoke about vague non-existent projects. By putting up a facade of being super busy when you are not, people try to lie to a world that frankly doesn't care. I have seen too many people become bitter and resentful, never coming to terms with the fact that their option A was not available to them. It is better to work out a good option B and make the best of it. But turn to option B only after you have explored every way of making option A work.

Even those who have made it to the very top of their professions are not spared by guilt. It is interesting to see successful women who are aggressive and ambitious at work get very defensive and insist that they do a lot at home as well. To the outside world, it might appear that they have it all, but strangely, even this species lives with the fear that having only worked all their lives, neither do they have any interest in domestic activities nor have they cultivated any hobbies. When work ends some day, they fear they will not know what to do with their time! Top achievers who invest considerable time and energy in their careers often do so at the cost of neglecting their own health and fitness. All those who aspire to look great when they make it to the cover pages must be conscious that all work and no workout is not such a great idea after all! Fitness is a way of life, and if it isn't adopted early, it could result in guilt later in life.

Keeping Guilt at Bay

There are many landmines in a career spanning thirty-five to forty years, and while no one is immune from guilt, some seem to manage it better than others to emerge winners. To my mind, a winner is a person who feels happy and fulfilled. They maximize the opportunities that come their way and become the best possible versions of themselves. They are at peace with the choices they make and have a sense of joy and fulfilment. Knowing what one wants helps one in being comfortable with the decision. Having a say in the decision gives you ownership of it. Sometimes we don't have the luxury of making a choice; life just hands it to us. You alone know your circumstances, your needs and your comfort level, so don't get caught up with what people say. Make your choice your own. Those who overcome guilt or know how to keep it at bay emerge as winners and I see that they have a few things in common.

A defining feature of a winner's mindset is that quitting never crosses her mind and that is largely because she doesn't take any decisions when she is upset or emotionally vulnerable. It is no secret that the worst decisions are taken when the mind is stressed. When the emotions settle down, she realizes that her problems, however difficult they may seem at the time, will pass, and for that to happen, she starts looking for solutions. She feels stretched, she gets hassled, she loses sleep, but she never considers quitting. And that is because she knows that her journey is a long one and some turbulence along the way is to be expected.

Being focused on your ambition means that you are clear about your priorities. Guilt, as I am never tired of saying, is an integral part of a woman's psyche and much of this guilt stems from ambivalence. I am sure we have all had passing moments when we have envied homemakers, thought that being single is an attractive option, imagined a life without pesky kids to be so much easier and so on. There will be days when we find ourselves overwhelmed by issues, and the temptation to throw in the towel would seem a convenient solution. In any case, a non-working mother or wife is a very convenient thing for the husband and kids! Once you too start believing that, quitting becomes a foregone conclusion.

Trust me, whatever your status might be—unmarried or married, with or without kids, a homemaker or a high-flyer—there is no escaping guilt. Being clear about your priorities and accepting the choices that follow make it easier to manage the guilt.

Winners learn to let go of what's not important and they are not hard on themselves about what they are not good at. A lot of energy is spent in trying to please everyone and being better than the others at everything. My friend Jaya is a chartered accountant and a fun person. Early in her marriage, Jaya's mother-in-law commented that Jaya made terrible tea. Most young brides in Jaya's place would have felt offended, taken the criticism to heart and held it against the mother-in-law for the rest of their lives. Jaya, who doesn't really enjoy housework, just told herself that this meant she wouldn't be in charge of making the morning tea! I am not suggesting that Jaya shouldn't have learnt to make a better cup of tea or that this is an easy way to duck responsibility. Sometimes, despite trying your best, you may not be as good as someone else at something. Your husband's colleague's wife might be a better cook or have a better done-up home. Just accept it and focus on what you are good at. At the end of the day, you need to feel both happy and fulfilled, not bitter and restless. Here again, a thick skin acts as an insulator from guilt.

Winners are great planners. Even when they have their arrangements in order, they have a plan B and a plan C ready. As Indians, we are always worried that something will go wrong and as working women, we cannot afford it at all. So there needs to be a backup or fallback plan for every single thing.

The only problem with this kind of efficient planning is that the home can run perfectly well even when you are not around. Women who come back from a tour to find that everything worked like clockwork in their absence start feeling redundant. The domestic help was so well-trained that the lady of the house was not missed at all! There is no escaping guilt for the female species.

1) Think of a situation where you allowed guilt to get the better of you. Is there any way you could have prevented it?
2) Think of a situation where you hung in and let the problem pass. Just smile and pat yourself on the back.

Chapter 5

Allies and Enablers

Kanchan Jain is managing director and head of credit at Baring Private Equity Asia. She has made it to the top job in an industry that is highly competitive and male-dominated. When I met her, I was amazed to see how close she comes to people's image of a woman who has it all. After a degree in engineering and an MBA from IIMC, Kanchan has had a thriving career in investment banking, enjoying the many challenges that came her way. She has worked out of India, in Hong Kong and London, is a mother of two, heads a largely male team and maintains residences in London and Gurgaon. A globetrotting lifestyle, a rewarding career and a loving family, what more could one want? I asked her how she managed it all.

'You can't have careers without help,' she says with a straight face. She has no doubt that managing both work and home would have been impossible without support from her parents, in-laws, husband and, of course, her domestic help. 'Sometimes you need to pay through your nose, at times you need to compromise, you might even need to reach out to others for help,' she says, having experienced it all.

What Kanchan says is absolutely true. You can focus on your career wholeheartedly only when you have the peace of mind that comes with an efficiently run home and reliable care for your young kids or aged parents. A reliable and fail-proof support system is therefore a prerequisite to a successful career. It is your best insurance against feeling guilty at work.

The Support System at Home

Unlike in more developed countries, we don't have great infrastructure such as crèches or old-age homes to look after either kids or the aged. At some level, the idea of sending them to such facilities does not go down well with the cultural sensibilities of a large section of our society either. As a result, the most common support system in large cities is paid domestic help. Nothing resonates with the sisterhood more than when I say, 'Behind every successful career woman there is a maid.'

A good and reliable maid can be the single biggest contributor to a woman's career especially when you don't have family support. I would like to believe that many successful careers have been built on the shoulders of these women who step out of their own homes to run the homes of career women. Treat your help with respect, pay them well and be sensitive to their needs.

No wonder then that the maid, over time, becomes an important part of the family and her employer pampers her and even brings her gifts from travels abroad. Our mothers who have grown up on a staple diet of Ramu kakas from Hindi films, who remained simple and loyal and worked with the same family for decades, are shocked to see this new breed of domestic help that is upwardly mobile and can't do without television serials or their own mobiles. This is a generation that learns new recipes (among other things) from YouTube, which is why one of the first questions when they join you is to ask you for the Wi-Fi password! Keeping your maid happy can often mean ignoring your mother's advice, and this can be a potential area of conflict if the parents are also part of the support system!

Growing levels of education and opportunities to work in commercial set-ups like retail outlets and manufacturing units have led to a significant decrease in the number of women working in homes for a living. Commercial jobs are seen as more respectable and if there are co-workers, the working environment is considered safer as well. On the other hand, the number of working women has steadily gone up, leading to a growing demand for maids. Hiring good help has become expensive and increasingly difficult these days. But the positives are that they can be trained, and since you pay them, there is no sense of obligation or guilt. Good help is hard to come by and so, just like women tend to hold on to good employers, they don't let go of reliable maids either! Retaining these maids becomes a huge challenge, and there are women who even claim to offer them loyalty bonuses over and above handsome salaries. A trained maid who you can manage to retain is a huge asset and no less valuable than talent that you want to reward and retain at work. Depending on how busy your schedule is and, of course, the affordability, some spare capacity is also advisable so that you are not stranded when someone from your domestic staff falls ill, decides to leave or is out of action for any other reason.

Look at the support system as an investment, not as an expense. The extra maid and air tickets for parents to fly down in case of emergencies, seem worthwhile when you look back and see how they contributed to your career. Women can fall into the trap of wondering whether the job is worth the struggle, especially if a considerable amount is being spent in day care or on help for the kids or elders.

One of the reasons why it is more challenging to run a home as compared to an office is that you deal with staff who don't always understand the importance of your work, commitments or career. At work, we deal with teammates who are aware of and respect your calendar and commitments. At home, there are times when the support system threatens to collapse at the most crucial juncture and one's nerves and HR skills are tested to the maximum. Despite that, every woman has stories of how she felt helpless on a big workday and how she coped. I have conducted group discussions while the field staff entertained my young son. Smita Affinwalla, presently an HR consultant, used to be in financial services earlier. She tells me of how she had tried for months to get an appointment with the chairman of the State Bank of India. The big day finally arrived but Smita woke up to find that the maid had bunked and she could not make alternate arrangements for a babysitter at short notice. Needless to say, the meeting with the chairman had one more attendee, Smita's baby! As mobile penetration has grown phenomenally, communication has become easier and cheaper. Hopefully, such stories will get fewer with every passing year.

Festivals, or holidays, are when busy career women make sure that they spend quality time with the family. Unfortunately, that is also the time when the staff would like to take their own annual leave. An out-of-the-box idea is to hire help from communities other than your own so that your holidays don't coincide. If your maid does not have her own family commitments at a time when your family is home for Diwali, or if your maid is free to work in the evenings when you are observing Ramzan, it's just that much more convenient and seems to work well for some.

When the maid is new or the children are young, women are more comfortable if the maids are supervised. This is where parents are often required to step in. Just having someone from the family supervise the kitchen and the kids can relieve a working professional of so much anxiety. However, as Dr Anita Patel puts it, 'In a joint family, you could barter the support you get for an inferior position in the family, where decisions get taken without consulting you, since you were away at work.'

Viji has always worked full-time and thinks a crèche is a good option, but many of her friends tell her that their in-laws are offended by the suggestion. Grandparents worry that society would assume that they are shirking their responsibility. They also get the feeling that youngsters don't believe they are capable of looking after grandchildren. That makes many young parents settle for the grandparents-supervising-untrained-maids option. Since the modern generation trusts Dr Google more than Grandma's traditional wisdom, that is a potential area of conflict. Viji knows young mothers who have quit their careers for this reason alone. I hope you remember the advice that Gauri got, 'When you have handed over your child to the mother-in-law, consider it as hers.' Now see how it makes so much sense!

Younger parents view professional crèches as more modern set-ups with qualified help. Some employers even reimburse for day care, making it a favoured option. Children also enjoy the company of other children, and somehow, being a paid option, it frees young mothers from the feeling of obligation towards either set of parents. Many employers now have this facility, making it a convenient option as well. You can go and check out the toddler or breastfeed the baby in the early days. However, most crèches are available only till the child is a couple of years old and the option works for those with fairly fixed and predictable hours. Children need looking after till much later, and so a crèche is a limited period facility.

I see a big business opportunity in the domestic house help space. There is a crying need for a service that provides trained and professional house help like cooks, maids, nannies and drivers. If you have an aggregator like Urban Company that provides masseurs, AC maintenance services, plumbers and the like, this could be the next most welcome step.

The childcare space is fast developing with players like Klay offering crèches and pre-playschool facilities. Clean and safe spaces, with trained nurses and teachers on board, is what builds confidence among parents. There need to be many more of these, dedicated ones attached to large offices or local ones on the lines of neighbourhood schools. Both these businesses need to get organized, with policies and regulation put in place by the government.

Post Covid-19, we find that many of these facilities have either shut down or become terribly expensive, since they have had to reduce their intake significantly to comply with social distancing norms. Good-quality, affordable childcare should be treated as an essential service and must be accessible to all. The pandemic turned out to be very hard on working couples with young children and arrangements needed to be rejigged. With a view to make working from home easier on parents with young children, many employers started paying for nannies instead. Didn't I tell you that work-life integration is a constantly evolving process?

When they get a little older, urban kids start going to hobby classes, creating a mommy network that can be tapped into during emergencies. With most women working these days, this requires both camaraderie as well as coordination. I have found this kind of network useful, right till the children's Standard XII level, when conversations move from playtime to tuition teachers and career options. Often, such networks turn into carpools, so having a reliable driver is a good investment.

Whatever be the home and childcare arrangements, enrolling the spouse in your crew should be non-negotiable. He is the best person to understand your professional commitments. If you don't have parents living in the same house who can take care of home and kids while you are away at a conference or travelling, it is inevitable that your husband will need to be co-opted into the arrangement. The general verdict is that while men do try to share the load, much of it involves following instructions and not taking primary responsibility for any particular task. This does not quite take that task off the wife's list nor does it equip the husband to do it alone, if required. The more efficient way of sharing the load would be to divide responsibilities based on ability, preference, natural leanings or individual schedules so that each spouse takes total responsibility for the tasks assigned to him or her.

Our relatives abroad seem to have mastered the art of doing this since kids there have long summer vacations and are most often sent to summer camps with both the parents going to work. Ferrying kids to and from such classes requires a great deal of coordination. Most couples try to ensure that at least one parent is at home at any given time. Synching calendars to ensure that both parents are not travelling at the same time is an activity that occupies much time and energy of working couples.

I must confess that I feel very jealous when this topic of synching calendars comes up. My husband covers cricket on television, so his calendar is dictated by the cricket calendar and he does not have flexibility with dates. As a result, despite being a doting father, his schedule does not permit him to be much of a hands-on parent and we have not had a chance to follow this synching routine. He wasn't around when both our children were born or when we had our interviews for their school admissions. While he has been a caring and involved parent otherwise, he wasn't a part of our daily routines when the boys were growing up.

I remember a particularly funny incident when my younger one was in Standard V and had just joined a new school. For some reason, the school had informed us that a particular day was to be a half-day and that the school bus would not be available. Therefore, we were supposed to make our own arrangements to have the kids picked up at lunch. The driver got a bit delayed and seeing that most of his friends had left, the little fellow panicked and called home. In those days, we used to have a home office and mobile phones had not yet arrived. Unfortunately, he got to the wrong parent (who was unaware of this change in schedule) and asked in a small voice, 'Papa, I want to come home. How can I come?' only to hear a rather puzzled voice say, 'Why do you need to come home at lunchtime? What are we paying fees for?' *What are we paying fees for* has become a meme for the family and continues to cause mirth to our sons who are both working professionals now.

Supportive Employers and Bosses

In February 2018, we got together for what was the first-ever IIMA women's get-together. It kicked off with a panel discussion that I moderated. As I sat on the stage waiting to start, I remember thinking to myself that this must be, quite certainly, the most empowered group of women in India. Funnily, I came home that evening more emotional than enlightened. It was apparent that the challenges that women professionals faced had not changed significantly in thirty-five years. While there was not much talk of harassment, unconscious bias still prevailed. There was much regret that women were still holding back. I remember a feisty young lady who ran a private equity (PE) fund expressing frustration that she needed to coax women entrepreneurs with brilliant start-up ideas to use up all the thirty minutes that were given to them to present. One of the big talking points during our discussion was good employer policies. There was a feeling that if there were more women in an organization, it was more likely to have more inclusive policies. There were strong for and against views on this hypothesis. Many spoke about how women need to check places like Glassdoor to find out how prospective employers treated women executives. There was a suggestion that B-schools need to have a diversity-related score for companies coming to campus for placement. It was obvious that corporate India still has much ground to cover here.

Being with a good employer is, without doubt, a very important factor in ensuring that you don't slip in your career. This is probably why one finds women changing jobs less frequently than men. A nurturing workplace environment is a bigger driver as compared to money. A supportive employer, an encouraging boss, a workplace that helps you grow, are not always easy to come by. So if you happen to find these, don't let go. Successful women figure this out early in their careers. They know a good thing when they see it and hence, hold on to it.

Women-friendly workplaces must be, first and foremost, safe places to work in. The #MeToo movement created a heightened awareness about sexual harassment in offices. Policymakers have now put in place processes and redressal mechanisms that are meant to ensure that women don't have to put up with unacceptable behaviour. Some organizations have gone to the extent of advising their male employees to avoid calling women employees to their cabins or to ensure that other employees are present whenever they need to have a meeting with a woman employee. Some other companies insist on booking separate hotels when male and female colleagues travel together for outstation assignments. Some of these practices can be awkward, impractical or simply inconvenient. Consequently, a fallout of this action is that some organizations, to avoid such stringent compliance issues, are simply choosing to not hire women. Policy issues that are not holistic in their approach or are merely one-off initiatives, however well-meaning they might be, tend to backfire and prove counterproductive to the cause of women. There is also the feeling that many genuine #MeToo cases have been quashed by the powerful men involved. Instead of encouraging harassed women to speak up, such instances, especially if publicized, leave the victim not only vulnerable but also unemployable for life.

It is also possible that post #MeToo, mentors, who are mostly senior men, feel uncomfortable to be seen in the company of young female mentees, lest it be misinterpreted. The only losers in this situation are the women themselves. Lunch meetings in safe and more public settings like large restaurants or even the office itself should be preferred, and if the mentors could have the same rule for both their male and female mentees, there would be no bias either.

A good boss is one who judges you fairly on your performance and without any kind of bias, someone who does not encourage *chamchagiri* or sycophancy. In fact, she/he should be a person who will encourage you and nudge you into achieving your potential and also stand by you in case any practice at work seems unfair.

When you are looking to return after a break or need a reference while switching jobs, having someone who is familiar with your work, believes in you and is willing to back you can be a huge asset.

Jagriti, with almost ten years' experience in the medical systems space, decided to start up on her own in a similar space. Three years down the line, she had to wind up her start-up and return to a job. 'Often, HR is not sure of how to account for start-up experience on your résumé. Since they go by standard templates, entrepreneurs like me didn't stand a chance.' That's when a good reference from one of her super bosses at her previous workplace helped her land a good job.

Women sometimes get into tricky situations while working in groups, especially if they are the only females. Getting ignored or overlooked, being talked down to or not being able to put forward ideas in a forceful manner are some of the more common issues that crop up. It is unrealistic to expect male buddies to 'understand your situation'. We have seen that even when #MeToo cases started tumbling out of closets, some men preferred to look the other way. So, when you find male allies at the workplace—men who call out sexist remarks or behaviour, encourage women to speak up or just make good listeners—they need to be valued and recognized.

In a perfect world, women would have been natural allies of their own species. The smaller number of those in leadership positions would serve as mentors and role models for those aspiring to get there. Their experience, having been there, done that, would create a path for others to walk on. Younger women would know about potholes to be avoided, as they would about ladders they could climb.

At one of my talks, I remember being asked a question by Anita Sanghi, a senior finance leader, who happened to be the most senior woman in an audience that included many young women, besides a large number of men. We got chatting later when she told me that she sensed what many young women from her team wanted to ask me but were hesitant to do so, so she went ahead and asked the question on their behalf. By doing that, not only had the young women got the answer to their question but they had also seen the self-assured way in which Anita had asked the question. Senior women, like Anita, need to show the way by asking and answering questions, taking the microphone or offering to make presentations. Often, women who have made it to the top focus all their energies on trying to prove that they are as good as the men. Women leaders need to also take the responsibility of paying it forward. Society has always pitted women against other women—it has not (until very recently) allowed women to celebrate each other. It is the responsibility of women in power today to be inspired by the progress made by women before them and create a platform for the women who will come after them. When women rally together as a sisterhood, then as women in senior positions reach critical mass, it will automatically work towards reducing the unconscious bias that they encounter. This will also help in breaking stereotypes and make their collective voice be heard. More women in decision-making roles would not only give more power to the pack, but it also creates effective organizations. Diversity in leadership perspective is integral to the success of any organization.

Good employers ensure that they create an environment in which their employees are able to give their best. Their policies are based on fair practices that are employee-friendly. They take care to see that good managers don't leave easily. It is always a good idea to stay with a fair and familiar organization, especially at a time when you need some leeway. Changing jobs around the time you plan to have children can be potentially dicey as you might not have built equity yet with the new employer. Falguni Nayar tells me of how she stuck to her decision of not changing jobs till her twins were three years old. A big, new opportunity saw a number of her colleagues move but she decided to stay. Like a batsman looks at the playing conditions and chooses whether to attack or defend, a woman too needs to evaluate opportunities based on her phase in life.

There are a number of efforts being made now to ensure that there are interesting second innings options for women coming back from longer breaks. These involve not only upskilling initiatives but also a fresh onboarding exercise to help them settle well and regain their confidence. Neha Bagaria runs JobsForHer, an online portal that helps activate women's careers. She has helped many women who had taken breaks to get back to corporate life. Neha makes it a point to mention to the companies that she works with, that the candidates she recommends come with the requisite qualifications, have fire in their belly and need no notice period to join. Hiring them makes business sense; it is not towards a social cause. Working from home offers the hope of a comeback for a large number of women who dropped out of their careers because of long commutes that made working hours seem even longer.

Neha is very passionate about her work, and when we discussed the issue of how long the ideal maternity break should be, I found that she had a formula ready. 'Three months' maternity leave followed by three months' paternity leave!' she says. I was taken aback by this novel solution but at one level it made sense. Childcare needs to be a joint responsibility and there is no reason why a woman needs to bear the responsibility alone or feel guilty about it. Having a child is a cause for celebration and raising children must be given the same importance by society as earning for the family. Young mothers learn to look after their babies; there is no reason why young fathers should not be able to do it.

Most large offices have pumping rooms that help ensure that babies in the attached crèches are not denied mother's milk. Countries like Indonesia and the UK even have breast milk couriers that mothers who need to go to work can use. This kind of infrastructure helps not only babies but also new mothers who otherwise feel guilty about returning to work. Proper handling of maternity leave can be the mother of all game changers!

Leadership and Advocacy

S.V. Nathan is a partner and the chief talent officer of Deloitte India. Nathan has a keen interest in the development of women leaders. He was conferred the National 'Male Ally Award' by Avtar and Working Mother in 2017, for his stellar role in the development of women professionals and for supporting their cause. Nathan believes that for any leader to make a difference, they need to make the development of women leaders their personal mission.

'What you need to do to make sure that you have more women coming into the workforce is gear the rules towards equity, not just equality. Equality says that one-size-fits-all, whereas equity makes room to extend support that certain groups need to level the playing field. For instance, if there were a man and a woman and everybody felt that they were absolutely on par across all objective criteria, then can you be a little more subjective and choose the woman, because you don't have an equitable share of women in the leadership pipeline? The background being that today, when we start off from campuses, the gender break-up is almost equal at 49 per cent women and 51 per cent men, but by the time they come into junior management, it drops to 27 per cent women. It continues to taper to about 14 per cent and by the time it gets into the realm of leadership, it is just around 9 per cent.'

Nathan's observation is that due to a combination of cultural factors, social conditioning, and conscious and unconscious bias, women, unlike men, find it difficult to stake a claim to what they want. They also feel awkward about showcasing their good work. The change he sees is that the younger entrants into the industry are able to speak their mind. 'As a stereotype, self-promotion is not considered a feminine trait and is frowned upon, which goes hand in hand with the conditioning to downplay their achievements and their inability to navigate office dynamics. This can be a big weakness since organizations have unstated expectations and demands of employees,' he observes. Nathan feels that women can be helped to work with these unsaid rules by sponsors who can make sure that the right opportunities come their way and see that they are guided along to navigate a firm or an organization.

Based on Avtar's research on the impact of career enablers on retention and advancement of women in the 100 Best Companies for Women in India, the critical career enablers across career stages/levels are:

a) At the entry level, an inspiring peer group and structured women's networks made a significant difference.

b) At the mid-career stage where exits are most common, flexible working was the most critical factor. The impact of mentoring is also felt in the retention of women in managerial stages.

c) At the advanced career stage, mentoring is seen to be a critical enabler. Companies with well-designed mentoring practices see far lower attrition than those without.

In the study, women, too, ranked mentoring as the most effective enabler for career success. In the context of this study, mentors were experts who were typically senior to mentees (in terms of experience and tenure), who guide the women professionals on charting their career trajectories. Navigating challenging phases in their careers, including managing work-life integration challenges, becomes easier for women in the presence of an invested mentor.

The second most critical career enabler as voted by women is an inspiring peer group—an outcome of having structured networks for women. In an atmosphere where they are amidst like-minded professionals who inspire and motivate them in their career pursuits, women felt it is easier for them to handle career-related challenges.

The third most important career enabler was organization-led skill-building programmes—relevant in the context of continuous skill upgradation. This was especially true in sectors where technology plays a significant role.

We have talked earlier about how self-doubt or faltering self-belief is an issue many women occasionally grapple with. Unlike men, women going through self-doubt can't seem to cover it with bravado. When faced with a challenge or even an unexpected opportunity, the average woman, though equally competent, comes across as unsure, unlike the average man. At such times, having a boss who can nudge her, back her and show confidence in her, helps. Deepali Naair tells an interesting story of the time she was in a marketing role in an earlier organization. When another senior in the organization quit, her boss offered her a challenging customer service role in addition to her existing role. 'But I have never done anything like this,' was her first reaction. 'He was surer of me than I was!' she says.

Eventually she learnt the ropes, worked hard and, in her own words, did a damn good job. Thinking back, she says she was lucky that she had a boss who believed in her. Often, organizations are unable to distinguish between competence and confidence, so being committed is not enough; you need to appear confident as well.

For years, we have had male brand managers for cosmetics or sanitary napkins, but you will rarely find a woman handling liquor or cigarette brands. Her response is more likely to be, 'I am a non-smoker or a teetotaller. How will I be good at finding consumer insights in this category?' The good news is that this is changing rapidly in India and that is a good sign. The CEO of Diageo, the liquor giant in India, is a woman!

I have always believed that women can learn from the larger and more diverse pool of men. Having supportive male mentors and advocates can help women see their shortcomings and get over their inhibitions.

* * *

Shabnam and her sister were the only girls from their family to go to college. Today, they are both well-settled professionals. Initially, their parents faced barbs from the extended family about how the girls would get spoilt with all that education going to their heads. However, seeing the success of his daughters, Shabnam's father has now become a strong advocate of higher education for women.

I also shared the story of Jagriti, who felt she was cheated of her performance bonus because of her maternity leave. Jagriti and her husband were shocked by the shabby treatment that a star employee like her was put through. Her husband, a top executive for another MNC, now goes out of his way to support the women in his organization to settle back in after their maternity leave. Yes, as Nathan said, 'In order to make a difference, you have to make it your personal mission.'

Many of the women I spoke with seemed to suggest that men know how to manage their bosses and other seniors better. While it is understandable that women tend to maintain the distance and formality of relationships, it is equally true that within organizations, you need advocates who will support and promote your ideas. This requires employees to be politically savvy, to figure out who could be your ally and whose voice matters. Understanding and navigating politics at the workplace is a useful skill to have and something that women cannot afford to ignore.

A few years ago, when Rishi Gour was country president of Sodexo in India, he won an award for Diversity and Inclusion CEO of the year. Sodexo is a French company where the promoter family takes an active interest in driving their diversity and inclusion initiatives. SWIFT (Sodexo Women's International Forum for Talent) is an advisory board dedicated to ensuring better gender balance at all levels of the organization, especially for leadership and with particular attention to P&L (profit and loss) positions. Rishi says that till he got invited to join SWIFT, he had never really given any professional thought to the challenges that women face in their careers. At home, of course, he was fully aware of how tough it had been for his wife, two years his junior at IIMA. Like a typical Indian husband, he had expected his Mumbai-based wife to move with him to London when they got married. She, too, like a typical Indian wife had dutifully followed him, without even a job in hand. After a frustrating three months of being at home, she did find a suitable job but very soon after, the company that Rishi worked for offered a big opening back in India and so they made plans to move back. After being uprooted for the second time, a maternity break followed, leaving the couple who started off with the same educational background and similar opportunities, with vastly different-looking career graphs a few years later.

Rishi vividly remembers his first SWIFT meeting. He was one of only two men in a group that had twenty-one women and felt seriously outnumbered. He confesses he was 'intimidated', never having been in a minority in any forum. Now he knew exactly what women experience in similar situations. It prompted him to take up a number of initiatives to improve gender balance in the company and pursue them with a deep sense of commitment. Rishi believes that while policy is an important requirement, it is a slow process and quite inadequate unless it is accompanied by intention.

'It needs to be driven like any other change management programme and the leaders should ideally see it through in their own tenure,' he adds.

Change begins at the top and Rishi made it a point to emphasize the importance of gender-balanced teams, repeating the message at every possible forum. It was made an integral part of every leader's KPI and in a few years, was also linked to 10 per cent of the leaders' bonus. This required relooking at hiring patterns at all levels. Walking the talk is always the difficult part, but people quickly realized that the company saw gender balance as a key dimension of leadership and started taking it seriously. It helped that three internal studies conducted by Sodexo over four years among its 50,000 teams with 4,25,000 employees worldwide pointed to a strong correlation between gender balance and business performance. Sodexo teams that had a 40–60 per cent male–female ratio did much better than those which were skewed. The business case had been irrefutably made and was being advocated and pursued by a strong, committed leader.

Technology and Time Management

A big part of success is how well you make use of your skills, and you will find that those who are achievers at work also bring their professional competence to other aspects of their life. Professional women are efficient homemakers as well. They may not be the best cooks or interior decorators but they see to it that their homes run like well-oiled machines. Technology is helping women, especially the young, tech-savvy ones, run their homes efficiently and manage their time better. Hiring domestic help is done with the same rigour as hiring talent in the office and innovative loyalty bonus schemes are devised to retain this talent! In spite of all this, there's always the fear that staff will ditch at the last minute and so, a plan B and even a plan C is put in place to take care of emergencies.

Technology is an integral part of the modern-day woman's support system. There are apps that help you order groceries, calendars that help you coordinate the children's activities, to-do lists and reminders on Google Calendar, Excel sheets to help you plan the week's menu, nanny cams, pet food vending machines and so much more. Young people are using their professional and managerial skills in running their homes. Life needs to be perfectly structured and organized, and the home needs to run efficiently. And when, despite all your efforts, something slips up, which it will, sometime or the other, learn to be okay with it.

In large cities like Mumbai, Delhi, Bengaluru and Hyderabad, apart from long working hours, people also have to put up with unbearably long commutes. Cutting down travel time, therefore, considerably improves work-life balance. My own office is a three-minute walk from home. This not only saves a lot of time and energy but in an emergency, it also helps me attend to the needs of the household, not to mention the luxury of having lunch at home. Anyway, the trade-off for having an office close by is that the rent is high but it is still worthwhile given that I save on travel time. When Rama Bijapurkar's daughter was just starting school, getting admission to a good school was a priority. The family settled for a much smaller house than they could afford so that they could be close to the school. Dr Anita Patel chose to run her practice out of a single nursing home rather than having multiple attachments with various hospitals so that she made the best use of her time and did not waste time in travel. Time is just as valuable as money for the working professional.

Finally, you need to be your best ally. If you watched Kareena Kapoor in *Jab We Met*, you might remember one of her dialogues. I certainly do because it brought a smile to my face.

'I am my favourite person,' she tells the hero and that defined her most endearing attitude in the movie. I find that those who succeed in life give themselves sufficient priority. They work very hard in their careers but don't kill themselves with the less important issues. They invest in domestic help, ask for support from their families and spouses, outsource whatever they can (cooking is top of the list!) and, most importantly, invest in themselves. That's not restricted to their careers alone but also extends to nutrition, exercise, networking and grooming. Yet sadly, I find a majority of women echoing Jagriti's lament, 'For a long time, I came last in my order of priority and time allocation.' That needs to change.

The two sexes view success through different lenses. Men are happy with professional achievements; it is what gives them their identity. A woman wants so much more from life. She sees her success in being an all-rounder and for that, she needs to put together a strong team of allies and enablers.

1) Identify your core and backup crew and see if they are adequately equipped to handle emergencies.
2) Identify and invest in tech tools that can make your life more efficient and stress-free.
3) Identify male and female buddies or mentors who can support you in fulfilling your dreams.

Chapter 6

Home—The New Workplace

My father-in-law, whom we called Bappa, was a professor of French in Hyderabad. He was always amused (and a bit worried) that neither Harsha nor I had regular jobs and would never get a pension. I have been self-employed for the better part of my life and so I set up an office from home, well before working from home became the norm. The idea that one doesn't leave home for work was itself alien to Bappa, coming from a generation that dressed formally to the single job that they held all their lives and was uncomfortable not shaving, even on holidays. Bappa and I had a fairly formal relationship, so around twenty years ago, soon after we moved into a new home, I was surprised to see him throw at me what seemed like a challenge.

Let me give you the background. When we managed to buy our own home in south Mumbai before we turned forty, Bappa was proud of our success. And I suspect a little less worried about the pension bit. While house-hunting, we had a condition that the new residence should accommodate a small home office with an entrance separate from the residence. We were delighted when we managed to find something that fitted the bill. It is not like we didn't run a home office from the old house but since we were already in that apartment before we decided to work out of it, we had to make do with using the room that was most convenient. Now that the requirement of a separate entrance had been met, he was curious to know how it would play out. Over the years, he had seen me juggle work and kids and wondered if the new arrangement would be any different. A small detail that I had overlooked but hadn't escaped Bappa's eye was that the office was bang next to my bedroom, so apart from the external entrance, there was a connecting door from my bedroom! Now he wanted to know if I would dress formally and have clear-cut office hours, or if I would just saunter through to the office in my home clothes, even late at night. Bappa was trying to get a sense of the exact challenge that we all are now facing with the more recent work from home (WFH) situation and so he challenged me with Rs 3000 thrown in as a bet! I don't know if he thought I won or lost eventually, because I never dared to ask!

The Evolving Face of WFH

Interestingly, being self-employed has been an older avatar of working from home. It is a general descriptor that covers a wide variety of occupations like freelance project managers, solopreneurs, part-time consultants, work from home content creators, among others. Over the years, it became very popular with women as it offered a better work-life balance compared to a full-time job. While being on your own leaves you without the security of a corporate umbrella, it allows you, at most times, the freedom to pick and choose your assignments and have the flexibility to decline an assignment if you have family commitments. If you are lucky, it could allow you the flexibility of running your errands while earning you a decent amount of money. You learn to be more efficient and pack in a hell of a lot, with no one around to disturb you. If it had not been for flexibility, I would not have done even half the things I managed to do in my career.

Watching my boys grow up has been immensely joyful. Having a home office during that phase ensured that I was there to open the door for them when they got back from school. Anyone who has brought up sons will know that a day in a boisterous boys' school is rather lively and full of action. Stepping out of the rowdy school bus into the security of the home also means letting go of pent-up emotions as a result of the fights and the bullying. Being there to listen to their stories about whom they fought with or who got punished, I found, has gone a long way into developing a strong bond with them. I stepped on the career accelerator and started yet another new venture at fifty. At the age of forty-seven, I started taking lessons to learn to play the keyboard. There is always time for everything if you know what your priorities are at different stages in your life.

Hema Mani heads HR at Lennox International and does a lot of work in the area of diversity and inclusion. When Hema's kids were born, she had great support from her parents who lived close to her home in Bengaluru. When her work took her to Chennai, it meant that she had to leave the kids to the care of new maids, something that she was not entirely comfortable with. When she contemplated giving up work for a while, her husband pushed her to go freelance and helped with the technology solutions that she required to set up a home office. The beauty of the new world is that for most businesses, a laptop and a mobile are really all you need to get started!

WFH became a more familiar term in the last decade or so but was mostly restricted to the technology sector. Since many large companies, particularly in the IT sector, are based in far-flung business parks on the outskirts of cities like Bengaluru, Pune and Hyderabad, they started the practice of offering WFH options for certain roles. Even organizations that did not have clear-cut policies in this regard made exceptions in the case of top performers. Like all new initiatives, WFH came with its own set of challenges, not only for the employee, but also the manager.

Around 2016–17, Pallavi worked full-time with a digital marketing company in Mumbai for about a year and then, when her husband switched jobs, she decided to move to Pune with him. She worked out a WFH option for herself and came to Mumbai only once in two weeks. It wasn't easy. The convenience of technology can never make up for the rapport that face-to-face meetings create. The nature of her business also required a lot of brainstorming in groups, some of which happens spontaneously and during informal discussions. Pallavi also thinks that employees working remotely, unlike those who go to the office every day, are less visible and therefore not always top-of-mind for organizations and can easily get overlooked. But she and her manager were committed to making the arrangement work. Not only did Pallavi join all the virtual brainstorming sessions but she also went through recordings of other meetings and texted and talked to colleagues frequently. Her manager, too, made the effort to keep her in the loop and ensured her work was recognized during appraisals. The WFH arrangement was possible only because she had already built equity and trust during the days she used to work at the office. 'You had to earn it,' says Pallavi. Her observations are, of course, from a pre-pandemic time when there were few employees like her who were allowed a WFH option on request, at least in her industry.

Now, of course, it seems certain that working from home will be a lasting legacy of the Covid-19 pandemic and even when companies settle down to a hybrid model, it will remain an option for most employees, at least some days of the week. Large employers like Tata Consultancy Services (TCS) have already announced that by 2025, no more than 25 per cent of their employees will need to go to office. A survey by JobsForHer reveals that even roles that were considered unquestionably full-time roles are being considered for WFH. Several organizations have announced that they are cutting down on office space. This only means that the new norms that have emerged, courtesy of the pandemic and frequent lockdowns, will become a permanent feature. A positive fallout could be that when a sizeable section of employees work from home, it is more likely that they will be treated on par with the full-timers.

The Pandemic—a Trailer for the WFH Experience

Making working from home productive takes a lot of self-enforced discipline. There are always so many distractions and little things that require attention at home, and with nobody really watching, it is so easy to slip into home mode and lose focus from work. For women in particular, the whole process of getting ready and commuting to work and back helps them switch from one mode to the other. The absence of that compartmentalization can be a struggle. So getting into work mode by moving into a demarcated space at a specific time and getting back into the home space to signify the end of the workday, can, to a large extent, serve the same purpose as the switch. It also helps send a signal to the kids or domestic help that when you are at work, you are not to be disturbed. This, by the way, turned out to be a major gender-related issue during the Covid-19 lockdown with many women wanting to take a sabbatical for a while. When women are at home, even working from home, the rest of the family would still like a piece of them, whereas the household help takes it as their right to interrupt for directions. The breakdown of that switch, which regulates work and office modes, can cause the same havoc as a faulty traffic signal at a busy crossing.

The biggest challenge around WFH is to simulate an office environment in a home situation. Creating your own office space is a must, and while working at the dining table was acceptable during the lockdown, it will not work as a long-term solution. Your office space needs to be sacrosanct, neat and tidy, comfortable and efficient. There is an amazing range of furniture, even space-efficient cubicles for small homes that emerged during the lockdown, thanks to some enterprising business folks who saw opportunity while people struggled to cope with the new realities of working from a home space. The office haven needs to be quiet, well-lit and with a steady Internet connection, given that all communication will be on the phone or the Net.

Women working out of smaller homes in cities like Mumbai struggled to create a dedicated office space at home. Once the novelty of working from home wore off, children walking into a virtual meeting started making for poor optics. Having kids and pets barging into a Zoom meeting might look cute in viral videos but not all bosses find the situation funny. Managers started complaining that the noise in homes made it difficult to carry out meetings.

The pandemic messed around with people's lives in many ways. As the lines between work and home blurred, pyjamas and slippers came to be all-day workwear. Comfort was the topmost consideration as style did not matter any more. Fashion websites reported an increase in sales of leggings, trainers and tracksuit bottoms. Every day became dress-down Friday and folks let their guard down as large virtual meetings tended to be audio-only. While audio calls are more comfortable, in the long run, video calls are more effective in one-on-one discussions or small groups. They also help in making your presence felt, something that is going to be a challenge in a 100 per cent virtually connected environment. Face time and a direct connection with your team helps you understand each other better and goes a long way in creating stronger bonds. Managers, struggling to get work done remotely, are also likely to feel at ease watching the team on video, reassured that they have not dozed off!

One of the positive side effects of the pandemic was a renewed emphasis on home cooking, as families bonded over food and started having more meals together. However, the luxury of a hot and more elaborate meal compared to the office *dabba* can come in the way of switching back into work mode. On the other hand, since there are no formal or informal interactions with colleagues that normally happen in an office, one could end up sitting in a chair doing video calls for too long unless you force yourself to stretch or stand or get up and walk around every hour or so. In the absence of office rules and decorum, great self-discipline is required to be productive and efficient.

HR folks have been positioning WFH as being great for flexibility, something that millennials crave, but there is a real chance that the lines between work and home get so blurred that your work-life balance goes for a complete toss.

Aishwarya is a consultant with a Big 4 firm and one of many youngsters who had to curtail their wedding festivities and settle for a low-key celebration during the lockdown because of the Covid-19 pandemic. It also meant that Ash and her husband Sid couldn't go on a honeymoon, as planned. I assumed, therefore, that in the absence of the honeymoon, working from home would be perfect as it would give them more time to spend together and get to know each other better.

'Earlier, clients at least threw in the customary "Sorry to disturb you over the weekend" line, but now they don't even bother with that,' she says. You are expected to be on call 24/7. 'When the lockdown was strict, you couldn't even say you had a family event or that you were on leave!' she laughs.

A woman's handbag and the things it carries have been a subject of constant amusement to men. It gives an insight into the variety of jobs that women handle and the extent of our resourcefulness. What we don't realize is that even when we go to work, we carry with us the remote controls to our homes and our children. Many women at the workplace use lunchtime to check things at home, give instructions to staff or follow up with the children. In a WFH situation, lunchtime and other breaks are no longer sacrosanct and work-life balance can, on occasion, get worse; not always better, as organizations would like to believe. WFH is being made out to be the panacea for retaining women in the workforce, but it is not that simple. Just having the lady of the house at home sees the entire family making demands on her. Most women find it difficult to say no to demands from loved ones and end up overstretching in the bargain. The mental switch, as I said earlier, is important for our sanity and when work invades the home, we need to draw the lines ourselves. No wonder there is a large number of women who prefer the routine of the office to the convenience of skipping the commute.

The energy and buzz in an office atmosphere is what is probably the hardest to replicate, even on video calls, which is why a hybrid model where all employees work from the office for half the week and work from home for the rest, is likely to emerge as the most popular model.

While the lockdown was an extreme case of what working from home could be like, it gave everyone a trailer of the multi-starrer. The myth that men were not efficient with household chores was busted faster than we had imagined. Families discovered that home-cooked food could be made just as interesting as restaurant fare. Parents and children actually bonded over simple activities at home. Single folks and young couples who lived on their own, moved back to be with their parents. All in all, much effort went into running the home but there was family support like never before. A large proportion of women found the lockdown experience refreshing, but only once domestic help returned. Many enjoyed the helping hand that normally reluctant husbands and children extended. Those who were spared the long commute actually found time to exercise or try a new hobby. The most stretched, I suspect, were parents with young schoolgoing children who had to endure the additional burden of supervising online classes and also keeping the children engaged.

The Downside of Flexibility

While flexibility is great and probably the primary reason that so many women look to WFH for part-time options, it is possible that every assignment that you turn down comes with the risk of missing out on future opportunities the same client or assignment could have paved the way for. Flexibility also cannot be the reason for compromising on the quality of work. You could choose to work for two hours, four hours or ten hours, but at all times you must stay committed to excellence. If career is a priority, then keep in mind that the inability to travel or attend conferences or courses can shrink your professional network and have a negative impact on your career in the long run.

Dropping out of the rat race is an acknowledgement of one's inability to keep up with the work schedule that the world demands. The rat race involves constantly benchmarking yourself against others to see how well you are performing or if there are areas where you need to improve. Conversations with colleagues keep you sharp and constantly updated about what the others are working on or how they are investing in themselves. That happens naturally when you work full-time in a proper office environment. The absence of this benchmarking can steadily dull part-timers; it is a risk that is not always apparent.

When you are self-employed, you need to be just as professional as anyone who works for an organization. Your work needs to be thorough, deadlines need to be maintained strictly and you might need to spend from your own pocket on software, hardware, industry reports and other things that enhance your output. In fact, the absence of organizational backing means that you need to try even harder to generate business or deliver to satisfaction. Those working for themselves, too, have reputations to maintain!

While being self-employed and working out of home allows you to manage your day better, the flip side is that you could go through very lean periods when you have no projects coming. Being a one-woman army (which is most often the case), you need to do all the work yourself and that includes rather mundane jobs like doing your accounts and even couriering documents; things that typically other people do when you work in organizations. You crave for the network, the office lunches and the gossip. Having run a home office for close to two decades, I can tell you that to run it like a truly professional outfit requires a great deal of discipline. It is very tempting to slack off instead of learning something new when you have nothing urgent lined up. The trick is in recreating the office experience.

If you have decided to work freelance or part-time for a bit because your kids or elders need attention, know that it is temporary and avoid getting into bad habits. Afternoon siestas or binge viewing, for example, while being immensely enjoyable can be addictive and are difficult habits to break. Going back to a regular job after you have been self-employed for some time can also be tough. I know a number of people who believe that they are most efficient and productive when they work alone and struggle to get back and work as part of a team. Getting used to the routine after having had the taste of independence requires adjustment and can even be difficult.

WFH—Opportunities in the Post-Pandemic World

As things limp back to normal, we find many jobs lost and several businesses shut down. With increased safety concerns and social distancing norms, support systems like crèches have either shut down or have become more expensive. Early reports suggest that more women have lost jobs during the pandemic, compared to men. So, while there are some new opportunities, there are also new concerns. Only time will tell how things will pan out for women and how many will choose to make home their new workplace.

As I write this, we have still not completely recovered from the pandemic, and an extraordinary event of this kind has the potential to change the world forever. It seems very likely that working from home in varying degrees will become the norm as a large number of people will work on contracts, not be employees of companies. Their skills will define their role, and unlike today, they will be recognized by their role-based personal brand rather than the companies they are associated with, quite like specialist T20 players who have specific skill sets for which they are selected to play in different leagues all over the world. Technology and good Internet speeds will help the trend of being location-agnostic become more implementable. Digitalization of many sectors like education, healthcare and media will rapidly accelerate, making many services go online and opening up a large number of opportunities to work from home. The gig economy will be here sooner than we think. It will bring a lot of opportunities that would be in the nature of projects or assignments instead of regular jobs. As people go from assignment to assignment with possible gaps in between, work life may cease to go on in a linear and continuous fashion, giving legitimacy to interrupted or irregular careers. Traditionally, women who wanted to return to work after a break had to justify or feel embarrassed about gaps in their résumés, but that could well become the new normal. However, in such a situation where there is no job security, constant upskilling and reskilling would be critical for many job profiles. Communication, public relations (PR) and the power of negotiation will be the individual's responsibility and therefore essential skills to get assignments. Typically, these have been seen to be female limitations and they will need to be worked on. Flexible work hours, part-time opportunities and WFH options for professional women could prove to be potential game changers but only if women approach them smartly.

- Those who work from home miss these aspects of going to the office:
  1) Dedicated and distraction-free time for office work (whatever the number of hours you choose to work)
  2) People interaction and learning opportunities
  3) A return to home life after office work is done

Find ways to improve productivity, focus, networking opportunities and commitment to excellence while enjoying the flexibility of working from home.

- Since it seems most likely that workplaces will follow the hybrid model, organizations need to find ways to keep WFH employees included, engaged and productive.

Making WFH Effective

The secret to making WFH effective and productive is to try and recreate the office atmosphere at home. It does not matter whether you work full-time, part-time, a few days of the week or temporarily from home.

1. Allocate a specific, dedicated space as your workplace. It should ideally be a room or at least a desk. Your family and domestic help need to be told that when you are at work, you are not to be disturbed.
2. Get organized. Give all instructions to the family and help before you get started.
3. Try to stick to fixed work hours. Dress for work. These help in mentally switching on and off from work.
4. When on conference calls, see that you don't always keep the video off. Getting sufficient face time with your colleagues and boss is important for team bonding and building trust.

5. Invest in office furniture, technology, industry research, etc., to ensure productivity.

6. Use free time to read material related to your work, enrol in online courses, etc., to keep yourself up to date. If you are disciplined and committed to excellence at all times, it helps getting back to working from an office, in case that is required.

7. Keep lunch light and quick, especially if you plan to continue working after lunch.

8. Divide household responsibilities among family members so that you don't struggle to complete your workload.

Chapter 7

The Diversity Agenda

It was only in the late nineties that the insurance industry in India was thrown open to private players. This was a huge opportunity for local banks and global insurance companies, and consequently for other potential gainers like advertising agencies. Till then, Life Insurance Corporation (LIC), with its ads saying, 'Save for your son's education and daughter's marriage,' had been in a monopoly. Times have changed since, the messaging looks dated, but no one had pushed the market leader to think afresh. With the private insurance brands entering the market, here was a chance for ad agencies to do some great communication in a hitherto unexplored sector that was expected to see much action. That the new brands came with bigger budgets was an added incentive. I was still in advertising then and part of a pitch to a rather large private insurance client. There was much excitement around the table when the first set of advertisements created by the agency's creative team was to be reviewed by the rest of us in the team—account servicing, account planning and media planning folks. A big part of the strategy was the visual—a stunning red bindi that was smudged, which the creative guys thought was a subtle and creative way to indicate that the policy took care of the family in the event of the death of the husband. While the men around the table had this 'We have cracked it' look on their faces, I, as the only woman present, was completely taken aback. As it is, insurance is what is known as a grudge purchase—one that brings no joy to the buyer—and this creative treatment brought up the worst kind of imagery. Which family, however practical, would warm up to an insurance brand that triggered imagery as morbid as this? Fortunately, I have never been one to shy away from speaking my mind, so I pressed for a dipstick study that included men and women. The study confirmed my fears and the creative team went back to the drawing board. What seemed like a mere product to one group could have deep emotional connotations for another, and missing out on a critical input could have been a disaster for the agency.

Gender diversity is not merely about having women in the workplace but about ensuring that the viewpoint of a significant and increasingly influential section of society does not go unrepresented. For most consumer businesses, it makes common business sense to have feminine insights since it is women who make a majority of the decisions in many homes. They may still not have as much say in their husbands' transfers or their investment portfolios, but most organizations would agree that today, the 'consumer is queen' is more appropriate than the 'consumer is king'. Factors like greater globalization, increased mobility and mixed marriages have contributed to greater diversity in most markets. With the emergence of newer, more influential consumer segments, having breadth in thought and perspective within your own team is important, as it invariably leads to better decision-making. Post Covid-19, as we try to reimagine businesses, the workplaces of the future, and indeed life itself, organizations that stick to a monochromatic way of thinking and problem-solving will inevitably find themselves vulnerable in the long run. The same is true for doctors, engineers, chartered accountants, lawyers, architects and all those who cater to the needs of a community that has a sizeable if not equal proportion of women, a segment that is increasing in its influence.

A Business Case for Diversity

Diversity initiatives need to go way beyond compliance. Since the pool of talented and qualified women is large enough in most disciplines, meeting the mandated numbers is not an issue. Sectors like media and advertising, or even IT, FMCG and pharma, actually see healthy numbers of women getting in at the entry level. It is the alarming dropout rates along the way leading to low levels of women in decision-making and leadership roles that is the issue. The more recent addition of an E for equity to the diversity and inclusion (D&I) agenda is a direct result of the fact that for diversity and inclusion to succeed, first there is a need to create fair opportunities and a level playing field for all.

Inclusive workspaces are decidedly more cohesive and productive. Organizations committed to diversity, equity and inclusion (DEI) are more likely to become employers of choice. A number of studies also suggest that organizations that practise D&I deliver better financial results. A McKinsey study titled 'Diversity Wins' (2019), for example, finds that companies in the top quartile for gender diversity on executive teams were 25 per cent more likely to have above-average profitability than companies in the fourth quartile—up from 21 per cent in 2017 and 15 per cent in 2014. Clearly, more diverse companies are better placed to win and retain top talent, improve their customer orientation, score higher on employee satisfaction and display better decision-making. All that leads to a virtuous cycle of increasing returns. Clearly, the case for diversity needs to be viewed as a business requirement, not merely a politically correct HR initiative or a policy that needs to be complied with. In his speech on 15 August 2019, Prime Minister Modi talked about building India into a 5-trillion-dollar economy by 2024–25.[5] Would it not be a waste if a large number of trained professional women do not get the opportunity to participate in this plan and contribute to the nation's growth? Green initiatives are rewarded with carbon credits and the like; organizations are incentivized to contribute towards improving the environment and engage in corporate social responsibility (CSR) activities. A similar initiative to encourage diversity would be entirely worthwhile.

A diversity agenda certainly helps women get into organizations, but if we need to retain them and see them grow into leadership positions, a culture of inclusion is imperative. Generally, while MNCs are more progressive on this front and also have global compulsions to commit to best practices, you will find that many organizations fudge figures or indulge in dishonest practices. They make up the numbers by hiring women in departments like HR, IT support or communications. Having women in roles that are neither revenue-generating nor client-facing makes them vulnerable when the company decides to downsize. Many more women are said to have lost jobs during the Covid-19 pandemic for this very reason. For DEI initiatives to succeed, there has to be real intention and commitment from the top. One of the ways this can happen is by making it a part of a leader's KRA (Key Responsibility Areas) or rejecting candidates for leadership positions if they fare poorly on this score. Leadership styles must be assessed not only on the leader's drive and delivery but also on how gender-liberal and inclusive he/she is. Secondly, a detailed analysis of how many women have quit, at what stage and for what reason will shed light on whether it is domestic issues, unfair work demands or a difficult boss that are responsible for the leak in the pipeline. Women talk about toxic bosses as a big reason to quit. Are bosses held accountable for this? Is there a redressal mechanism for the subordinate or a counselling programme for the boss? The women probably find it easier to simply quit that job and look for another, but should not organizations view this as a failure to retain talent? Anjali Mohanty feels that a strong and fearless HR head can do wonders in creating the right culture. She feels that HR heads need to be the conscience keepers for the management, calling out unacceptable behaviour and introducing fair and healthy practices in the organization. If the war for talent is for real, businesses simply can't afford to neglect what could be nearly half their talent pool.

A diverse workplace comes with its own set of challenges. Along with ensuring representation for minority groups, organizations need to make sure that their voices are heard as well, otherwise the whole exercise would whittle down to mere tokenism. A great example of making the diversity agenda work to the benefit of all groups is the Indian Premier League (IPL). IPL franchises bring together cricketers from different countries, races, age groups and economic backgrounds. The IPL is one of India's strongest brands not only for its commercial success but also because players from all over the world look forward to the tournament as an opportunity to interact with and learn from others. A heterogeneous group is most conducive to learning, provided the power dynamics within the group are managed. A situation where freshers have to play alongside stalwarts can be a tricky one and requires sensitivity on the part of leaders. Paddy Upton, who has been part of several high-performance teams, including the Rajasthan Royals, says he spent considerable time and effort managing team dynamics. He particularly encouraged younger players to speak up. If they had shared any ideas with him in a smaller group, he would mention them in the larger team meetings. This gave the youngsters a lot of confidence and a feeling that their contribution was not insignificant. Women, too, are often shy of speaking up in larger forums and fear being ignored or overlooked. Encouraging them to express themselves can help boost their confidence and get in their valuable inputs.

The results of D&I finding a place on the corporate agenda are already beginning to show, with workplaces increasingly looking more gender-friendly. While people in general work longer hours, organizations are taking care to see that women employees reach home safely. Larger organizations have childcare facilities like crèches, apart from flexible working hours for young mothers. Maternity leave is at a more generous six months. There are several WFH options. We can see many changes that earlier generations fought for, are making it easier for women to enter and stay in the workforce.

Ensuring the safety of women is a non-negotiable requirement for workplaces. That includes arranging drop-offs if they are required to work late, providing proper arrangements in case they need to travel and, of course, seeing to it that they are not harassed at the workplace. Prof. Punam Sahgal is ex-dean of IIM Lucknow and is a leading expert in organizational behaviour in the country. DEI is an issue that is as close to Punam's heart as it is to mine. A paper published by Punam Sahgal and Aastha Dang in 2017, titled 'Sexual Harassment at Workplace: Experiences of Women Managers and Organizations', attempts to understand the occurrence and dynamics of this horrible experience that some women go through at work. It seeks to explore how women manage such behaviour meted out to them, and what kind of policies and processes organizations have for protecting them from being sexually harmed. It makes an interesting distinction between the more serious but less common sexual harassment and the more rampant and less obvious sex-based harassment.[6]

The #MeToo movement brought into focus sexual harassment, where a number of men in powerful positions sought sexual favours from younger, more vulnerable female colleagues. It encouraged women to unite and speak up about what they went through in the past and the present. The Vishakha guidelines had already been stipulated by the Supreme Court in 1997. #MeToo created greater awareness throughout the country, more episodes got reported and publicized, and there was much discussion around what behaviour was okay and what was not. Several large organizations put in place policies, practices and redressal mechanisms to handle any cases that got reported. Unfortunately, sexual harassment is like betting in cricket—everyone around is aware that it happens but it is very difficult to prove in court. As a result, court cases have gone on for long, organizations have tried their best to protect the powerful predators and ultimately, the court judgments have been far from encouraging. This has left women somewhat disheartened because while they are named and shamed, made to answer the most uncomfortable questions in front of committees and forced to quit to escape embarrassment, there is a good chance that the men escape without much damage. The paper quotes research that shows that organizations with better co-worker solidarity and grievance mechanisms have a greater rate of reporting but also questions whether legal measures are sufficient to curb this menace. Besides, every compliance requirement comes at a cost to organizations. Those that are not committed to DEI prefer not to hire women rather than cause inconvenience to themselves.

Sex-based harassment, on the other hand, is more to do with men using their gender power to put women down. Passing sexist remarks, making offensive jokes, are things that men have enjoyed for decades but now, in the new and more equal world that we live in, are totally unacceptable. Sensitization programmes are helping men understand unconscious bias. Prof. Sahgal's paper, based on the responses of 800 women, also found that women who become targets of inappropriate behaviour of colleagues first blame themselves, think it is their own fault and wonder if they have brought it upon themselves. Some also downplay the incident, wondering if they are overreacting to what is a commonplace occurrence. They make concessions to the offender like saying that he could have misbehaved under the influence of alcohol as he is otherwise well behaved. Perhaps women tend to safeguard themselves by denying or discounting the importance of such experiences, which may, unfortunately, send signals that they do not have misgivings about being treated disrespectfully. As Prof. Sahgal rues, 'We have educated our girls; they are career-oriented and are financially independent, yet they seem to be locked in the patriarchal mindset.'

Diversity Needs Equity and Inclusion

What started off as a movement for equal rights for women has now matured into a call for greater equity. Equality is about treating all people the same but equity involves acknowledging, understanding and accepting differences and seeing how companies can benefit from diversity. At the end of the day, women are different in that they have different needs. That does not make them less equal. What it does require is that we relook at systems that have traditionally been designed keeping only men in mind. Sometimes, some amount of tweaking makes a process or policy compatible across genders, but at other times, the issue needs to be addressed with new eyes. I remember reading interviews of a number of women who broke the glass ceiling in various sectors and they all had amusing stories about how when they joined work, there were no toilets for women. Typically, offices in the old days had the wall-hung urinals that catered to an all-male employee base. Now, no amount of changing the height or size or number of these urinals would make them suitable for women; you just need differently designed toilets! While women did get toilets specially made for them, the minor modification solution seems to be a popular approach when trying to make things inclusive. There are also several issues like safety, sexual harassment and maternity leave that are faced by women alone and their inputs must be taken into consideration while framing policies.

There is a growing realization that diversity without inclusion has no meaning. Since bias is the primary reason for non-inclusion of minority groups, many organizations are putting their employees, both male and female, through sensitization programmes to help them understand unconscious bias. As the term suggests, often the behaviour of individuals has less to do with mala fide intent but is rather a by-product of patriarchal conditioning and systemic sexism. Interestingly, men report that these kinds of programmes at work are eye-openers and help them on the home front as well, as they start appreciating their wives more. Many mothers find their daughters calling out their fathers for sexist remarks or treating their mothers unfairly. There is a greater chance that fathers would listen to daughters than to wives, which is what makes this all the more encouraging in our efforts to create an equal world.

Deepali Naair tells an interesting story about how even women can be guilty of unconscious bias. In 2016, when she was on a break, she and a colleague were planning a CMO conference and started drawing up a list of invitees. When the entire list was done, they noticed that there were no women on it. In this age and given her personal commitment to diversity, someone was bound to point it out. It was not as if there were no women CMOs. Some of them were less visible women and, therefore, not top of mind. They needed to be consciously included.

'No one ever says they don't want women; sometimes it is just unconscious bias,' she says. 'Just like when you are looking for carpenters or drivers, the first names to come to mind are male.'

The only answer to break this stereotype is to have more women in these positions so that they are more visible. More women on interview panels for selection and promotions will also enable a fairer chance for women candidates. Asking the question 'Why don't we have enough women?' in as many forums as possible will help keep the issue alive in the collective consciousness of the entire organization.

In fact, this process needs to start even earlier than the workplace. While we rejoiced in the statistic that 25 per cent of the IIMA batch is made up of women, I was aghast when Prof. Promila Agarwal mentioned to me that less than 1 per cent of the case studies that are used in class had women as protagonists! I am happy to see that this is now being corrected.

It is not as if men don't want to have more women as colleagues. It is just that they are not inconvenienced in any way by the existing system and its unspoken rules. Changing it in a way that it becomes more inclusive is too much of a bother, something that will require considerable sensitivity and personal initiative. Currently, most men are happy being 'mentally feminist' and believing that all is well with the world.

Measures to Bring about Real Change

Introducing practices that prevent unconscious bias and ensuring a level playing field are two ways by which organizations can advance their diversity agenda. Hiring on the basis of blind CVs, where the name and gender of the applicant is hidden, is one such practice. Target recruitment, which involves taking care that while hiring, you include colleges that have a large number of women, is another. Consciously ensuring that women get to face a variety of challenging roles rather than making allowances that they don't need or assuming they won't be able to do it is yet another. Correcting the imbalance in a system that is geared essentially towards men would itself do half the job. For the rest, some amount of corrective action might be required if we want to hasten the process.

Ideally, all policies should be screened through the diversity lens to make sure that they are free from any bias and offer equal opportunities. In this day and age, it is unfortunate that there are instances when women have had to demand equality.

I have observed that younger women are more idealistic and are dead against any kind of 'favours' like quotas, lower cut-offs, additional marks, etc., that some organizations and B-schools are experimenting with in order to meet diversity targets. Older leaders like Roopa Kudva, Rama Bijapurkar and Anjali Mohanty are more pragmatic and say that they have come to realize that affirmative action of some nature, at least till the time we have sufficient numbers, would be necessary. Creating a level playing field is a slow process; fighting years of sexism is going to be a challenge and without any kind of intervention, it will be an uphill task.

As executive coach Promila Ayyangar puts it, 'Culture building is an art and a science. The policy initiatives make up the science and while that is necessary, it is not sufficient by itself. Policy initiatives demonstrate the intent of the leadership, no matter how often their implementation falters due to intangibles like the unconscious bias of the various people involved in implementation. Leaders need to be sensitive and willing to be vulnerable to accept such failures in order to not be in denial of these roadblocks. That is the art element.'

'The veil of social conditioning is still indeed too heavy to move by just softer approaches,' she feels.

Rishi Gour has been a champion of gender balance at the workplace. He too feels that a policy of no discrimination, no allowance is not fast enough to show results and there is a chance that the leader who drives the initiative would move to another role or even organization before he can see it through. Rather than merely relying on the pipeline, he has successfully experimented with tangential hiring to include women from outside the sector. The first step was to not close an opening until a few women had been interviewed. Secondly, while he would normally insist on competencies, attitude, aptitude and relevant experience for men, for female candidates, he would relax the condition of relevant experience. This opened the pool to include competent women from other industries. It, of course, meant a lot more time investment to coach and mentor them while they made the transition, but it was a very effective way to achieve gender balance. 'To start off, all my six P/L heads were men, but in about two and a half years, the scorecard read a happy 3–3,' he proudly shares.

'Like any other change initiative, DEI needs to be in the top three agenda points of the leader,' says Rishi. 'If you get busy with something else, even for a quarter, you will find that progress has halted.'

At Sodexo India, where Rishi was country president before he joined Theobroma, he ensured that women with promise had exposure trips to their headquarters in Paris where they got to meet influential seniors. That led to opportunities to work on global projects. When visitors from overseas came to the India office, he made sure that the women here had face time with them. A leader can be proactive in ensuring equal opportunities to even the less pushy groups. 'After all, the leader controls the agenda and gets to decide who gets access and who doesn't,' he says with a smile.

In August 2015 in the US, then President Barack Obama put the spotlight squarely on the need for more workforce diversity. He issued a call to action to technology companies, encouraging them to hire more women and minorities by implementing the Rooney Rule. The Rooney Rule requires 'at least one woman and one under-represented minority be considered in the slate of candidates for either every open position or every open senior position'.

Originally implemented by the National Football League (NFL) and named after Pittsburgh Steelers' chairman Dan Rooney, the original Rooney Rule sought to increase the opportunities for minorities to hold NFL head coaching positions. While there were enough black players in the NFL, there were very few black head coaches. The results of applying the rule were impressive—minority head coaching hires in the

NFL increased from 6 per cent to 22 per cent in 2006. Over a dozen major technology companies, including Facebook, Amazon and Microsoft, responded to Obama's call and committed to ensuring more diverse recruitment and hiring practices. The McKinsey study 'Diversity Matters' (2014) showed that ethnically diverse companies are 35 per cent more likely to have financial returns above national industry medians and gender-diverse companies are 15 per cent more likely to do the same.

The diversity metrics used in the implementation of the Rooney Rule capture data at three stages—who is being interviewed, who is moving to the next stage and finally, who is getting hired. It is a good framework to ensure that all minorities get representation at the interview stage and also gives organizations a clear picture of the stage at which the drop is happening. Over time, the correct diagnosis can help the organization rectify the problem. The rule further attempts to see that the best candidate eventually gets selected. It does not sacrifice merit but ensures that no segment is denied opportunity or gets left behind. In that sense, this is better than a quota system where there is a chance that an undeserving candidate gets selected.

However, the Rooney Rule is a slow process and is still open to subjective bias. After ticking the box for the requisite diversity figures at the first stage, if the rest of the process remains unchanged, no change is likely to happen. As with any other compliance initiative, in the absence of true commitment to the cause, there is a good chance that it might be treated as just another technical requirement.

Sometimes, selection metrics themselves are skewed in favour of certain subgroups. Earlier, admissions to the IIMs used to be based on the CAT score alone. The exam itself favoured those with a high level of quantitative skills, leading to classrooms with 94–98 per cent engineers. With a view to having more diverse classrooms, the exam was made less quant based, and while the CAT score continued to have significant weightage, the candidate's marks at the Standard X and XII levels were also considered. This not only resulted in more women qualifying but also gave students from the arts and commerce streams a fairer chance. Internationally, there is a healthy trend towards constructing diverse classrooms. Teachers report that this move improves the quality of discussions within classrooms, bringing varied viewpoints on several issues. There is good reason for organizations to work towards constructing diverse teams.

The Role of Policy

Over the years, the government has taken policy measures with a view to prevent women from leaving the workforce. Since the maximum dropouts happen at the childbearing stage, it was believed that proper handling of maternity leave could be a game changer. In 2017, India passed the Maternity Amendment Bill that requires all companies with over ten employees to grant six months' paid maternity leave to their women employees. While six months of paid leave seems very generous, it is not as straightforward as it appears. Firstly, smaller organizations, small to medium-sized enterprises (SMEs), start-ups and the like find this unaffordable and, as a consequence, are unlikely to hire women in the childbearing age. That would rule out a large section of young professionals.

In larger companies, this has been a welcome move except that many women admit that a longer break means they are more likely to lose their current role or may get overlooked for promotions. While there is no fixed policy on paternity leave, the more progressive companies are offering paternity leave of between two and six weeks. Paternity leave can help equip a father with the skills required to become a hands-on parent and in doing so, ensures that the mother has more support from him when she gets back to work. Despite paternity leave being paid leave, the response has been poor, with a majority of men refusing it. FOMO at work is so great that men are happy to pass on the entire burden of childcare to their wives.

Babies need care beyond feeding. Inoculations and problems related to teething, for example, are spread over the whole year. If there is flexibility to take paternity leave any time during the first year, it might encourage men to take over some childcare duties. Instead of labelling leave as maternity or paternity, if all employees are entitled to a gender-neutral 'family leave', it might go a long way in signalling that the decision to have children is a joint one and that both spouses must share family responsibilities.

Another significant policy initiative is the introduction of a law that states that every company board must now have at least one woman member on it. Since the number of women in leadership positions is still small, this has even prompted some organizations to have programmes to fast-track women managers to get them into senior positions. Others have chosen to look outside of their own companies. Unfortunately, compliance-based initiatives often get implemented only in letter, not in spirit, and many a time actually do a disservice to the cause as a whole. Filling up boards with unqualified women from among family or friends doesn't further the cause of women nor does it improve the quality of boards.

Even where deserving women are appointed, 'at least one woman' is often interpreted as a single slot that needs to be filled. So, even if you find more suitable women, they are not considered, as the quota of one has been filled. *No less* is being read as *no less, no more*. A quota also means that even a woman who qualifies on merit is referred to by the disdainful expression 'diversity candidate'. Similarly, fast-tracking schemes too are not looked upon favourably by either women (who would rather qualify on merit) or by men (who feel cheated and disgruntled that they are not being considered).

No woman would like to start her career on the wrong note, and women on B-school campuses are wary of organizations that publicize their diversity agenda as some kind of CSR initiative.

Anamika passed out of one of the top IIMs in 2017 and was looking forward to an exciting corporate career.

'The only tricky situation I have had to face so far was during my MBA placements. A lot of companies that visit the campus come with a decided quota of "diversity candidates" they want to hire. A lot of these companies—especially with finance and consulting roles—do call female candidates for interviews first and the offers are rolled out. Typically, the girl students get placed in the first two days and sadly, the boys get placed later. Now the tricky part with this is that I believe the summer/final placements I got were because of my credentials; I was as qualified for that job just like one of my fellow male batchmates. But after the interview, I got the job and he didn't. I fully trust my capabilities of having secured that job, but somewhere there is that lingering doubt. Was that a biased decision by recruiters because I was a "diversity candidate"? Was that reverse discrimination? It is baffling how the provisions that are supposed to empower us are somehow causing that sense of self-doubt.'

If organizations are guilty of being insensitive in following the diversity agenda, women too are viewing this as an opportunity to grab board positions, irrespective of whether they can contribute or not. This again does nothing either to further the cause of women or add value to the board. 'Being on boards' is being made out to be a full-time occupation, and coaching classes for women to get on to boards have cropped up. Women who have made it to company boards on merit are deeply offended by these attempts that seem to suggest that only women need coaching to get board positions while men qualify automatically.

The problem really lies in the fact that the number of women who deserve to be on boards is currently small. While it is steadily growing, the women are either not well networked or not very visible in the media or in industry forums. Typically, when board positions are filled and other board members start looking around for suitable candidates, the old boys' network kicks in and only male names come up.

'Going through a headhunter with a mandate to have at least a couple of women candidates makes it far less biased,' suggests Roopa Kudva, who is herself on several boards.

The Way Ahead

Worldwide, the cry for diversity is growing louder and louder. At the World Economic Forum, 2020, in Davos, Goldman Sachs announced that it would only invest in companies that met the diversity criterion. Their CEO, David Solomon, said, 'Our goal as always is to provide our clients with the best possible advice to help them achieve their goals. An IPO is a complicated process unique to each company, but in some respects, it's rather simple: diverse leadership leads to better performance. Getting that right—before the IPO—is the right thing for all companies going public.'

The way ahead is probably for organizations to create a meritocracy where all talent is cherished and supported through equitable opportunities, along with a work culture that helps employees navigate their careers so as to meet their full potential. Diversity must be a desire, not a requirement.

Along with equality at work, we need equality at home where both spouses take equal responsibility of the home and kids with a vibrant support system that is reliable, affordable and easily accessible.

As you can see, there is no single remedy or game changer that will take us towards a fairer and more equal world, but it would need something more like a drug cocktail that is a combination of various remedial measures. Some are easy to introduce and can be done right away. Organizations, for example, can ramp up sensitization programmes on unconscious bias fairly quickly while the government, with support from corporates, can set up and regulate neighbourhood crèches.

Behavioural changes and newer mindsets on the other hand, will take much longer. There is bound to be some reluctance, some pushback, but we need to persevere. Many allies and ambassadors will be required to hasten the change and make a visible difference. Short-term policies like quotas will help accelerate the whole process and can be discontinued when the numbers look healthier. More than anything else, women must become strong enough to shape their own destinies and aspire to do more.

Organizations committed to a culture of Diversity, Equity and Inclusion must constantly check if:

1) They offer fair opportunities and a level playing field to all employees
2) Apart from complying with diversity targets, their policies and practices are put through a diversity lens and tracked to see that they deliver the intended results
3) Women are given visibility and a voice, and recruited in decision-making roles
4) They ask the question, 'Why don't we have enough women?' in as many forums as possible to help keep the issue alive in the collective consciousness of the entire organization

Women, especially in senior positions, must look for ways to strengthen the sisterhood and ensure that they provide fair opportunities and encouragement to younger women and those less privileged than them.

Chapter 8

The Equality Mindset

25 June 1983 was a big day for India as Kapil Dev and his team won the Cricket World Cup. That very day was another kind of win for me as my parents and I drove down from Mumbai to enter the hallowed gates of IIMA, where I was to join the PGP. By then, my parents, who didn't have a clue about management education, let alone B-school rankings, had awakened to the fact that their daughter had hit some sort of a jackpot and now wanted to make sure that she was safely dropped off there.

The first two days at IIMA were like a whirlwind—getting to know batchmates and dorm-mates, soaking in the famed red-brick campus and finding our way around the new dorm. Our batch of 180 had all of eleven women in it! One of the girls went home on day one even before we got a chance to see her, and another one dropped out two months later, bringing the already dismal count further down to nine.

On day three, classes started. The classroom was U-shaped and each seat carried a name tag. I was pleasantly surprised to find that we were two Kulkarnis in our section, Gururaj Kulkarni and I. While the seating was in alphabetical order, GD Kool, as he came to be known, didn't sit next to me. My seat was bang in the firing line in the centre, in row one, as my name tag said, Anita RK (Miss), while he was comfortably on the side in the second row as his read Kulkarni GD! A couple of weeks into the first term, once we girls got to know each other, we marched to the office and protested about this absurd discrimination. As it is, we were just 5 per cent of the batch size. Did they really need to rub that in? The PGP office said it wasn't possible to change the roll call at that stage but agreed that the (Miss) bit was quite unnecessary.

I am told the struggle continues despite the batch having over 25 per cent women. The name tags are now gender-neutral, but the email IDs continue to say (Ms) and carry the burden of bias. I don't know if the IT guys think it is an efficient way to sort data. What I know is that they continue to irritate a growing number of young women who are just waiting to prove themselves in the corporate world.

D&I has now become a mandatory part of the corporate agenda, and getting in the numbers at the entry level looks like an issue that can be resolved, given the steady rise of numbers into professional colleges in all disciplines. But diversity without inclusion does little for women as they continue to battle mindsets that hold them back and restrict their progress.

Much of this has to do with unconscious bias—unsaid rules and norms in society as well as misjudged assumptions about women and their abilities or their ambition. Women are constantly underestimated and treated as a separate talent pool.

Mind you, these mindsets are not limited to men alone. Women also are guilty of these notions of being a different category. After all, we are all products of the same social conditioning. The mindsets exist in organizations as well as homes and play out in a subtle manner on a day-to-day basis, often without us even realizing it.

When Nirmala Sitharaman became defence minister of India, it was a formidable achievement by any standard, but there were still those who ridiculed her by circulating old pictures of her at home, making pickle. Hillary Clinton and Kamala Harris routinely get trolled over their looks and clothes, as if that has anything to do with their accomplishments. Interestingly, the terms *career women* or *woman CEO* don't have male equivalents. And we only hear of 'mother of two' being used to describe a CEO, never 'father of two'.

The more unconventional the success, the greater the need for thick skin.

There are other topics like work-life balance, for example, that have been traditionally used only in the context of the female gender. Men, on the other hand, seem to only have busy careers to grapple with! This balance is a cause for concern not only to women but to the organization as well. 'How will you manage?' or 'Do you plan to get married and have a child?' are questions only asked of women. As with all bias, these questions evoke varying degrees of reaction from those on the receiving end. Some are more vocal in their protest against this behaviour and understandably so. Having children is just a natural progression in life and not some item on the CV or some blip on the career graph that merits discussion, they feel. The more pragmatic among us take it in our stride and would like to believe that the question is merely intended towards resource planning. After all, women do tend to relocate after marriage or need maternity leave when they decide to have kids, which, at a minimum of six months these days, is a fairly long time and needs to be taken into account and planned for by organizations.

Another stereotype that needs to be revisited is that of the devoted wife and mother who is willing to unquestioningly sacrifice everything she has for the sake of her family. Careers today come with serious responsibilities and financial rewards. A woman cannot or may not want to always follow her husband whenever he gets transferred, especially if such a move is going to put her career in jeopardy. Many husbands accept promotions that involve transfers without taking into consideration the wife's career prospects in the new location. Trailing spouses find it very difficult to find jobs in new locations unless it has been explored and planned in advance. Several of the successful women I spoke with have chosen to live apart from their husbands for a couple of years to pursue their careers. It is a difficult but necessary step, if you want to be fair to yourself. If the wife gets a fabulous offer but it involves relocating, would the husband be open to moving with her? That is still rare to come across.

The Role of Unconscious Bias

With the diversity mandate being pushed, which is a must, we need to ask ourselves several questions. What does it mean and take to be equal? Are we being treated as equals? Are we equal in our own minds? Do we behave like equals?

Promila Ayyangar, who also serves as an external expert on the sexual harassment redressal committees of a number of organizations, gets to hear many stories relating to gender bias. During one of the hearings, after the initial hearing of the complainant, a colleague of the complainant was called in as a witness. Her moving testimony threw light on the culture of the organization that covered biases and partisan behaviours of male leaders and colleagues way beyond the original complaint. The witness, herself a new mother, spoke about how on her return from maternity leave, she faced biased assumptions about her capabilities, priorities and commitment to work. She was taken off critical projects which she had been leading, not included in new project discussions and given back-end work, even though she was back full-time and had made ample arrangements for childcare. She also observed that when leaders decided promotions, they assumed that women with young children would not have time and so were not being considered for key roles. She quickly learnt her lesson and avoided referring to her baby in front of any office colleagues, removed photos of the baby from her softboard and underplayed motherhood, the biggest joy of her life. At the workplace, she had to behave as if her child didn't exist!

'While I could not hide my pregnancy, I hid my kid,' she tearfully admitted. She wanted to be recognized for her work and not be branded as a young mother (read incapable worker) whenever any conversation about her role or performance came up.

To be fair to the men, it is a possibility that some of them at least thought that by offering these women a reduced workload, they were being kind and considerate to young mothers. Many women would have even opted for a less demanding role for a while, when they returned from maternity leave, but this woman was not one of them.

So, rather than making assumptions about all women, the better way would have been to discuss the job requirement with the woman concerned and arrive at a joint decision. Sometimes, misdirected kindness can be strangely unfair!

If corporates maintain the discipline of examining every policy through a rigorous gender-neutral lens, that in itself would go a long way in minimizing unconscious bias and there would be little need to do anything that is specifically directed at women. HUL and ICICI are two organizations that are known for their initiatives on diversity and inclusion. HUL was probably the earliest to start a crèche in its Mumbai office premises. Interestingly, the crèche facility was received enthusiastically and availed of by its male employees as well. Anuradha Razdan, executive director, HR at HUL, says that all their policies are employee-friendly and gender-neutral. Along with six months' maternity leave, they offer three weeks' paternity leave as well. Flexible work options are available for men as well as women. In fact, HUL was one of the first to introduce a gender-neutral policy for survivors of domestic abuse. The culture is meritocratic and marries performance with compassion. All managers, men and women, are encouraged to step out of their comfort zone by being offered various global roles. I think it is better to create a culture where only talent matters instead of putting women in silos and viewing them as a separate stream with separate treatment.

'ICICI was run like the military where people were assigned jobs, not asked for preferences,' says Ramkumar, when I ask him how ICICI managed to throw up so many women leaders. 'ICICI did nothing special for its women, nor did the women expect anything special,' he insists. Like Anuradha, he too talks of a meritocratic culture with equal opportunities. But achievement comes at a price, he cautions, and the exemplary women leaders at ICICI asked for no concessions, instead creating robust support systems for themselves.

The symbols that we associate with power and success are money, designation, large homes and offices, employees at your beck and call, a jet-setting lifestyle and fancy cars. While these are male-driven, it is not that uncommon these days to hear or read of women who can claim to have earned many of these on their own steam. Yet, you will rarely meet women who brag about their salaries or their designations or flash their awards and promotions. Despite husbands being generally more supportive of their wives' careers than before, the woman earning more than the man is still a bitter pill to swallow, certainly in this part of the world. Under the circumstances, women feel it is wiser not to bring up the subject at all.

One of my close friends, Manju, is a chartered accountant married to an engineer. So, obviously she managed their money as well as the family portfolio. When she started earning more than her husband, she discreetly deposited her salary cheques in the bank and took care to see that her husband did not notice.

A younger friend, Rita, had an even stranger story to share. She married a guy from just one batch senior to her. Now they work in the same sector but in different companies. Being a year ahead, the husband earns just a little more than her. Rita's mother-in-law, for some unknown reason, thinks she earns one-third of what the husband earns. Since the mother-in-law is otherwise very supportive of Rita's career, she has done nothing to clear the misconception! While both

Manju and Rita seem relieved that they have handled their situations without rocking the boat, I feel sad that at some level they have been denied the joy and pride of their success by having to downplay their achievements. And that is only because they are women.

Along with conscious as well as unconscious biases that women have to put up with on a daily basis, there are systemic challenges both within family structures as well as at the workplace. Unless families, societies and work environments also change at the same pace, women will continue to remain disadvantaged. A woman without a choice or voice in the familiar environment of her home is unlikely to offer an opinion in a less-friendly context at work.

Equality at the Workplace

Equality is something generations of women have fought for. The call for equality has largely focused on equal opportunities and will continue to do so till a level playing field is achieved. While that happens, it's the responsibility of qualified women like you and me, who have already demonstrated our ability and desire by opting for a vocation, to hang in there and make a success of our careers. That will mean not only holding on to our ambition, but also not quitting or taking a soft option when faced with the slightest challenge. It involves unlearning any kind of behaviour that stands in the way of confidence and self-belief. This unlearning cannot be expected to happen overnight and needs to start in childhood itself. There is already an effort to move away from traditional fairy tales that portray little girls as weak and helpless beauties who need a prince to come and save them, to more assertive and independent portrayals. Films and serials with strong female protagonists help in reinforcing the equality mindset in both young boys and girls. Most importantly, the privileged among us must do what it takes to be considered equals at every stage of our careers, without asking for any allowances or having any sense of entitlement.

'Put your hand up for difficult assignments,' suggests Garima Dikshit, IIM Lucknow 2006 and a mother to twin daughters.

Women often choose or get hired for corporate office roles in big cities as they are considered safer and with better amenities. Not surprisingly, organizations also believe that it is less risky to give women assignments that involve more regular hours in office environments.

Priya Narendra, IIMC, 1992, works for *Hindustan Times* and is aware of unconscious bias that organizations can display when it comes to roles that are considered male bastions.

'It would help if organizations consciously ensure that women get to face a variety of challenging roles rather than either making allowances they don't need or assuming they won't be able to do it.' You need to have done the hard yards and ticked all the boxes before you are considered for a leadership position.

'I always opted for the most difficult and non-glamorous assignments, ones no one else wanted,' says Madhabi Puri Buch, formerly a banker and now the first-ever regulator from the private sector. 'It's a simple demand and supply issue,' she says. 'If you want roles that no one else wants, you are automatically valued by the organization,' is her strategy, and going by her success, it seems to have worked!

Putting potential leaders through different assignments is a powerful way of identifying leadership mettle. 'Most businesses have their leaders take up roles in various functions like sales, supply chain, operations and technology to develop leaders who understand the guts of the business. Without doing these stints, it is hard to be considered,' says executive coach and former chief learning officer at Wipro, Abhijit Bhaduri, offering an organizational viewpoint. For CEO positions, general management experience is preferred over specialist roles. Veterans in marketing will tell you that they have all been through sales roles and factory postings before they settled down to marketing. And this, traditionally, is where women have fallen short.

Ramkumar too warns against cherry-picking of roles. He finds that there is a category of women who refuse roles with travel, late working hours or those that involve front-end sales and then complain that they were overlooked when it came to leadership roles. 'You need to qualify to be a business leader, to be a CEO. If you haven't handled a P&L business, you don't qualify.' To drive home the point that the issue is of experience and not gender, he adds, 'As head of HR, I didn't qualify to be the CEO of the bank either.'

Women too must opt for challenging roles, especially early in their careers when family responsibilities are few, since exposure to a variety of roles will help build a strong foundation for your career. Besides, compared to the hardships that previous generations put up with, better infrastructure and connectivity in smaller towns have ensured that life has become much easier.

Given all the discussions regarding how to retain women in the workforce or why we have so few women leaders, one would imagine that the issues are more at the workplace—gender discrimination, a toxic work culture, sexual harassment

and the like. While this may be true to an extent and some
women may have had unsavoury experiences, the unanimous
verdict is that the challenge at home is bigger than the
challenge at work.

Equality at Home

*'It isn't the mountains ahead to climb that wear you out, it's the
pebble in your shoe.'*

—Muhammad Ali

Those of you who have played a sport like badminton, tennis
or table tennis will know that the skills required to be a good
singles player are not enough to be part of a successful doubles
pair. While ability and passion are obviously common to both,
the doubles pair needs a good level of understanding and a
great deal of mutual trust. The two partners have different
but clear-cut roles, yet on a day that one partner looks a bit
off colour or tired, the other should be able to carry the extra
load. I think marriage is exactly like that and when both the
spouses are working, trust and respect for each other become
even more essential.

When Madhabi Puri Buch was offered the position
of full-time member of the board at SEBI, she and her
husband Dhaval were in Singapore. While it was a great
opportunity for Madhabi, the couple were faced with the
prospect of a long-distance marriage which could extend
over many years. They worked out a plan by which they met
on weekends either in Mumbai or Singapore. Madhabi and
Dhaval are dear friends and when they told me that they had

managed to meet on fifty of the first fifty-two weekends, I was staggered by their discipline and commitment. You could always argue that they were privileged to be able to afford it, but I believe that if you have the will, you can find many ways to make things work, not all of which require money.

Kanchan Jain tells me that whenever she has had to choose between a great career opportunity and family responsibilities, her husband has always encouraged her to put work ahead of family. Despite having an equally demanding career, he assured her that he would hold the fort while she was away.

The spouse can either be an enabler or a speed breaker depending on whether he is willing to share the responsibility of home and family equally or not. The general feeling is that women are more invested in the husband's career, whereas husbands are supportive as long as their own careers and lives are not affected. Husbands who say, 'It is your decision,' probably don't want to get involved. A true partner would take real steps to see that the other is not denied equal opportunity.

A question I have been asked every so often is about my experience of having my spouse as a business partner. Most people see the arrangement as convenient while others think it must be awkward and wonder who is the boss. In the era of entrepreneurship, many couples foresee working together as a possibility for the future. Couples who are doctors, architects, engineers, lawyers, chartered accountants, too, can see this happening. To be honest, my personal experience has been a bit different from the professional one. As a couple, Harsha and I are both low on ego and high on trust. This is most important in a partnership. We have our roles cut out and we were clear right from the beginning that I would run the business. While we have never had any major disagreement, it was understood that should there be a difference of opinion, my call would be final. Since the business was built on our complementary skills, there was no occasion to tread on each other's toes. Professionally, however, there have been a few irritants. Not everyone is ready for a world where the wife runs the business. Those who don't know the couple think that either the husband is very sweet and is allowing the wife to take decisions or the wife is very aggressive and wants to hog all the credit. Either way, the woman gets the short end of the stick! In our case, a part of the problem was also that Harsha is a well-known name, face and voice, but even other partners seem to run into biased individuals who assume that the wife either helps or supports the husband. I have observed, among other couples, that initially, if the kids are young, the husband fronts the venture, taking care of sales, media interactions or funding. He becomes the face of the organization, and the organization, in turn, becomes known as his outfit. Once the business becomes big and successful, it is too late to change this perception. Young women who dream of starting businesses must be conscious of this problem.

Except for women who manage to build considerable domain expertise and a formidable résumé before taking a short maternity break, most others stand the risk of getting sidelined and seeing their career graph dip in some manner. Unless they are allowed to grab good opportunities that come their way later in life, they will never get a chance at catching up and stand the risk of always remaining distant second earners. True equality demands that every career move for both the spouses takes into account the implications for the other spouse's career. Earning power alone cannot always dictate every family decision.

If spouses were to take turns at prioritizing their careers, the man could need to compromise his career from time to time and, as a result, could meet with somewhat lower success as compared to when his wife would have constantly taken the back seat. I wonder how many men would be willing to do that. I also wonder whether a woman's conditioning would allow her to find the idea of a less successful husband attractive! Our conditioning is so deep-rooted that it makes changing mindsets really challenging and, as you can see, there are no sure-fire answers.

Women from my generation, now in their fifties and sixties, went into marriage assuming it would last forever. It was understood that it would be the woman who would have to make the most adjustment. That is what the family and society expected. The idea of 'the complete man' came a bit later. Today's young girls are not satisfied being the supporting cast . . . they would like to be leading ladies. And I don't see any reason why they should not, as girls are doing all the things that men did, including taking on financial responsibilities. Young women today are clear about their need for financial autonomy, and want to be equal partners in sharing expenses and contributing to buying a house. As more women jump into careers, they need support from parents, and often it is the girl's parents whose help is sought in managing the home and kids.

Traditional-minded parents are not comfortable living in their daughter's home, certainly not for an extended period of time. Women believe that if they co-own the home along with their husbands, it goes a long way in creating an equal status for them as well as their parents.

Disparity in earning between the spouses has the potential to alter the power dynamics at home. The widening of the gap diminishes the share of voice of the lower earner even further. They find it difficult to justify their time away from home as they feel that the money earned by them minus the money spent doesn't make it worthwhile.

The argument is flawed at two levels. Firstly, household expenses should be looked at as a percentage of the total income of the household, not the woman's salary alone. Besides, money isn't the only reason why women work. So when you quit, you are probably giving up your entire career, your qualifications and your professional worth along with your earnings of a couple of decades in the future, not simply the month's or year's salary alone. At such times, just hanging in there and waiting for the tough phase to pass is the best advice anyone can give you. In any case, never quit when you are emotionally vulnerable. Sharing your problem with others could lead you to new solutions or at least make you realize that you are not the first person to face such a problem, and encourage you to carry on.

Demanding Equality

The gender wage gap has been a long-standing issue all over the world. The degree varies across geographies and across professions or sectors. Normally, this is attributed to the fact that men negotiate harder, but I suspect that it also has to do with the problem that women don't seem to be comfortable demanding more, saying that they deserve more.

Chitra Ranade, a senior executive with a pharma multinational, offers an interesting insight. 'You can retain men by offering them more money. Women are unlikely to leave because the increment was low, especially if they are otherwise happy with the work culture.' While it is true that money is not the main driver for many women, it is important to keep in mind that your salary is an indicator of the value that the organization attaches to your work, and it is not okay when that is compromised.

'Even more so than men, women look for peace of mind that comes from working in a harmonious work environment,' says Rishi Gour. Poor work culture affects men far less. If everything else is okay, women are less likely to change jobs on account of a lower bonus and also less likely to get tempted with the promise of a big salary jump.

Sreevidya, a successful entrepreneur who has been in multiple senior leadership roles in different IT companies, is feisty and single. She was once asked in an interview why a single woman needed so much money!

'I too run a home and have a family I would like to support,' shot back Sreevidya. While personally, her individual expenses may be low, there was no way she was settling for anything less than she deserved! 'Shouldn't salaries be based on talent and the responsibility an individual is willing to take up?' she questions.

She says sometimes single women may not have a direct family to support, but they act as a backbone for an extended family or actively support a social cause or charity.

'Many a time women themselves are responsible for this lack of parity,' she says.

'Why this shying away from responsibility at home, while expecting to be treated equal in everything else?' Sreevidya asks. 'It is an interlinked social structure and empowered women need to be equally responsible for the change,' she feels.

It is odd, when even women who earn well think of themselves as secondary breadwinners. It is even worse when organizations assume the same.

The IT sector is supposed to be notorious when it comes to negotiation. In IT circles, the saying goes, 'The crying baby gets the milk.'

In firms that have offices in the US as well as in India, when someone shies away from negotiating, they are considered humble in India, but interpreted as lacking in confidence by the US office.

For men as well as women, the motivation to do well in your job and have a long and wonderful career comes from how you and your work are valued. If you wake up in the morning energized to go to a stimulating workplace where you are fairly treated, you will be inspired to give your best. When your family and you feel that through your work, you are making a difference to your organization and to your family's well-being, you will have a sense of being valued. Men don't have an option but to go to work, regardless of how much they enjoy it. Many professional women have husbands who are already earning enough to ensure a comfortable lifestyle for the family. If such women don't feel happy or fulfilled at the workplace, dropping out would definitely look like an acceptable option to them. Neither is there stigma attached to staying at home nor much regret that a career has been prematurely aborted. You will see this dichotomy in play at home as well.

Behaving like Equals

While it is entirely a personal decision, the way a couple manages their income gives a deeper understanding of how they view their own careers. Frequently, women suggest that their salary is like jam while the husband's is more bread and butter. The woman's salary is seen as a bonus and either splurged on holidays or saved and invested, mostly by the husband. While this might just seem like an accounting practice or even a fun thing to say, there is an underlying assumption that the woman's salary is secondary. The fear then is that her career, too, is treated as being more dispensable. I was stunned to hear women in high-profile jobs say that even during the years that they earned more than their husbands, they continued to think of themselves as secondary breadwinners! When we don't think of ourselves as equal contributors, there is hardly any chance that others would perceive us that way.

Even in the most progressive families, our cultural conditioning is patriarchal. While fathers in nuclear families are less distant and feared compared to earlier generations, they continue to be the ones who take all the major decisions. Domestic helps still believe that the sahib is their employer, the one who pays the salaries, while memsahib is in charge of giving instructions regarding domestic matters. My friend Alpana got a taste of this fairly recently. Alpana and Samaresh are a batch couple like Harsha and me. Marrying a batchmate is probably your best ticket to having an equal relationship, and while career graphs of the spouses may look quite different, the relationship remains largely equal. Samaresh, in this case, has had a more regular corporate career while

Alpana's career had a slow start but picked up really well once their kids grew up. Now, Samaresh is a consultant and works out of home while Alpana heads her own venture and works out of an office. The maid, however, continues to call and disturb Alpana for the smallest of things, but won't ask Samaresh, who is in the next room!

Alpana tells me how even in the most equal relationships, social conditioning and the idea of traditional gender-based roles can make an appearance when parents and guests are around. While parents are uncomfortable seeing their son or son-in-law do household work, the woman, who is normally okay with it, also starts feeling awkward in the presence of his or her parents.

I clearly remember an incident when we were invited to a friend's place for dinner and discovered that the husband had cooked an interesting three-course meal for the guests. It was so beautifully made and served that all the female guests went gaga and told the hostess what a lucky girl she was. The men, if only jokingly, told the host that he was setting a bad precedent and that their wives too, would now expect the same from them. The most interesting reaction was from the hostess who insisted that this was only a one-off event and that the husband did not do this regularly. Women seem to have transitioned into traditionally male roles quite easily, but men doing stuff around the home is still seen to be a step down.

It has become fashionable (and politically correct) for men to praise their wives in public. Most men acknowledge their better half's role in their own success. They say they are proud of their wives who manage home and careers so efficiently. Women too believe that men have changed to a certain extent, but mostly in theory. Their words suggest they are feminists, but not their actions. Home, hearth and children continue to remain the primary, if not sole responsibility of women. Unwell children, absentee maids and ageing parents are issues that bother women much more than they do men. 'I never realized at what point the maid and the home became only my problem,' says a niece I have seen grow up and who is now a mother of two.

'My maid was the pivot around which my world moved. If she came late, my whole day would go for a toss,' says Vinita. If the maid did not turn up, that was all she would end up thinking and talking about all the way to the office. Strangely, her husband, who travelled with her in the same car to work, never quite understood why the maid was the centrepiece of their discussion.

Over the last few decades, we find that women are taking over work that was considered traditionally male, like driving, financial planning or even home repairs, in addition to continuing to look after the home and children. The glaring flaw in women's lib, as we now realize, is that we have brought up our daughters to be like sons, but we haven't brought up our sons to be like daughters!

Oscar Wilde may have been ahead of his time when he said: 'All women become like their mothers. That is their tragedy. No man does. That is his.'

Equality is not only about being treated equally but also about behaving fairly as equals. When I started out, I had a senior colleague who was considered a high-flyer, someone youngsters like us were supposed to look up to. She and I found ourselves working late on a project at precisely the time her husband called to say that he wanted to end their decade-long marriage. I was young and inexperienced and had no clue about what one is supposed to say to someone in these rather peculiar and emotional circumstances. In the days that followed, she told me that she would have to move out of the home that belonged to the company her husband worked for. At the same time, she also mentioned in passing that they ran the home with his money whereas her salary was untouched and, in fact, invested in its entirety by her father! Besides not being an ideal partnership, that is hardly the kind of equality that previous generations have fought for.

More than anything else, an equality mindset is about being fair and positive. Successful women never make their struggles a gender issue. Women have special challenges but so do men, often more than the women. There is a realization that even the last-ditch option of quitting in the face of extreme circumstances is only available to women and there is no social stigma attached to it. Men need to hold on to their jobs and find it difficult to switch even when they have abusive bosses or work that they don't enjoy. Women in sales jobs invariably get to handle bigger, safer markets and doctors often get hospitals with slightly better facilities.

I have always maintained that to get treated equally, we must first ensure that we deliver our 100 per cent. When we do our jobs well and on time, we will not give anyone a chance to say that we left early or compromised in any way. To be able to do that consistently, even the most committed and efficient ones would require the support of someone who is a partner in the true sense of the word.

A Suitable Boy

What kind of a husband then does an ambitious woman require?

Rama Bijapurkar chooses an interesting term, 'gender liberal'. With the experience of a married and ambitious daughter and several married nieces, she is fully acquainted with the lifestyle of young independent-minded working couples and knows that there is no option but to share responsibilities. A woman cannot 'lean in', unless her spouse is equally competent to hold charge while she is away or busy. The more familiar scenario is that even when the woman does manage to work late or travel from time to time, she invariably comes back to a home full of complaints and jobs not done. The handover of chores, maids, kids, happens as soon as she steps in through the front door. My own decoding of a gender-liberal husband would be that he should have enough skill and willingness to run a home so that the wife doesn't feel the guilt of having neglected the home and family, quite the same way as wives with careers of their own do when their husbands are away on work. A marriage needs to be seen as a joint venture, a partnership where the show must go on when either partner is away.

Doorva Bahuguna cautions us against a tribe that she calls 'mentally feminist'. Her term is so exact and hard-hitting that I don't think anyone could have put it better. When I shared it with my husband, there was a smile on my lips and an oops on his. Doorva is a consultant who is focused hawklike on building brands and businesses and is equally committed to helping women succeed. By mentally feminist she essentially means men who would like to see their wives do well but have not given any thought to what kind of support they would require in order to succeed. I find that men have now smartened up to speak a language that is politically correct but when it comes to sharing the load, don't necessarily walk the talk. A majority of the time you find that men have never learnt to cook, do the laundry or buy groceries. Even when they decide to help, it is often about following instructions and doing only what they are told. They are smug in the belief that they do much more around the home than their fathers did, even if that doesn't count for much!

Fathers, brothers and sons too, tend to be mentally feminist and expect the women in the family to handle all domestic duties. I feel hopeful when I see the same men being openly supportive of their daughters' careers, when they had no guilt if their wives' careers were compromised. Like with all transformation, mindsets will take time to change, but the process will be considerably hastened if we have more ambassadors driving the change.

Is there any way then to figure out whether a potential spouse is truly gender liberal and not get fooled by the mentally feminist types? There is no foolproof test but there are definitely indicators or contributing factors like we had in checking career intentionality for women.

For starters, what kind of role models has he had? A good test would be to check how his father treats his mother. Do the women in the family get respect? Do they have a say in decision-making? Most people are influenced by relationships that they see around them while growing up. If a man has grown up seeing his mother or sister work, he would realize what it means to them. If the mother has worked, it is more likely she will understand the demands of the daughter-in-law's career as well as the importance of financial independence. If the women in the family have an equal say, irrespective of whether they earn or not, there is a good chance that he will always value his wife. The ones who say that their family is very forward in 'allowing' the women to work are the ones that are clearly problematic.

Arpita suggests that rather than trying to change somebody's view after marriage, it is simply easier to get married into a family that has similar views about the woman's career.

Dhanashree Shirodkar Joglekar, too, agrees that matching values is very important, but cautions us that the fact that he values education does not necessarily mean that he would appreciate a working woman as a spouse.

'In the initial dating phase, not many guys admit that they don't want a working woman. But if their reaction on seeing a working couple is: "Why does she need to work when he earns so much?" take the hint,' suggests Dhanashree.

Nimrat recalls an interesting conversation from her student days. An IIM batchmate she dated asked her if she would be cool being a full-time mom. When she asked him if he would be comfortable being a stay-at-home husband, if ever needed, he got uncomfortable and quipped, 'That's not how it works, no?'

My sister-in-law is married to a man who is very house-proud and also a superb cook. He has taken early retirement while she is still busy with a career that involves a lot of travel. Having a husband who is self-sufficient frees women of a lot of responsibility, and the resultant guilt. Their daughter-in-law, Pallavi, an advertising professional, tells me an interesting story about how she was sure about the man she decided to marry. While they were dating, she didn't fail to notice that Samir made it a point to ask about how her day went and also asked for her opinion while making decisions. When he came over to her mother's house, Samir would offer to help her mother in the kitchen or to clean up. When Pallavi and her mother met her in-laws for the first time, it was her father-in-law who brought out the tea while the mothers chatted. Now she had absolutely no doubt that his son would be both gender liberal and supportive!

The most common adjective in describing the dream spouse for a professional, far ahead of gender liberal and similar words in the category, is 'supportive'. Supportive comes in various shades starting from 'Is he willing to listen' to 'Does he share the housework' and 'Does he agree to hire extra domestic help'. Decisions like hiring extra help, buying expensive appliances or an additional car impact the family finances as well as time management. The spouse's active participation and understanding in such decisions makes matters easy. Here again, if the man has lived abroad or run an independent household before getting married, he could be expected to be more supportive (and competent!).

While wives are always expected to be supportive, a supportive husband is a pleasant surprise and women consider themselves lucky, bordering on grateful, if they have found one.

There is another kind of support that Indian women expect and Indian men struggle with. Indian parents are generally more meddlesome or at least have a greater say in what their children should or should not do. If the young couple decides to live separately and not with his parents, can he stand up to his parents and make them understand? If they plan to have kids late because that would be better from the point of view of her career, will he support her when she resists the pressure from the family? It would be a good idea to observe a prospective groom while discussions on the wedding arrangements are made. Does he have a view on what he would like and does he have a say in the matter or do his parents take all the decisions for him? The signals are there to see from an early stage; you only need to enter the relationship with your eyes open.

There were many unsaid assumptions, unarticulated expectations till now in society. It appears clear to me that urban Gen Yers are different. They are focused on themselves, surer of what they want and articulate their ambition a lot better. They don't assume that people will understand. Like most women, they are team players but they are clear that the 'I' must not get lost in the 'we'. A good spouse would be happy to see his wife retain her own identity and not expect her to merge it with his own. At the same time, if the 'we' part is not worked on enough, marriage can end up in divorce and that is a trend that is clearly on the rise.

Shweta Agarwal speaks for her generation when she says, 'The biggest thing a woman needs to watch out for is being undervalued. She needs to make sure that her prospective spouse and his family see her as an equal, as an independent woman who has her own life and her own mind. They should value her for her achievements and be ready to together build a life that both partners want, professionally and personally. My husband and I are from different communities and we struggled for two years to convince our families about our decision to get married. In one such conversation, a family member who was trying to dissuade my then boyfriend from marrying me told him, "She doesn't even know how to cook". He answered, "That's fine because I know how to cook and we can employ a cook, if required."'

One may or may not be lucky to find someone who can share the responsibility of the kitchen, but one must make sure one finds someone who wholeheartedly accepts that this is not a girl who is going to do all the household chores for them. This is a girl who is as educated and as capable as they possibly are and who has many peaks to conquer outside of the home as well. She, therefore, needs to have a conversation and set the right expectations. There will be days when he will need to wait for her to come back home long after he does, when he would need to talk her out of her tiredness, when she may not be available for all the social/family engagements, when he will need to baby-sit while she goes on work trips.

It is heartening to see that millennials are far more democratic and egalitarian compared to previous generations. The fact that the equality mindset is being discussed and demanded means that we have covered some distance. Agreed that there is a long way to go, but that is understandable. Much of the inequality stems from years of conditioning that cannot be expected to change overnight. While we should not be afraid to call out bias in our midst, I feel it would be more rewarding to gently and sensitively try and change one person at a time, instead of battling the world. As urban working professionals, we are definitely a privileged lot. Our voices have the power to make a difference. If we are fair and equal in all our interactions, it will automatically strengthen the cause. As our sisterhood grows, we will find strength in numbers. Our voices will grow louder, more confident and we won't be seen as the odd minority. Let us focus our energies on bringing up the future generation to respect and value the women around them. This way, we will definitely leave a better world for our daughters and their daughters.

In 2019, Falguni Nayar was awarded the Businesswoman of the Year at the Economic Times Awards for Corporate Excellence. She is a friend and batchmate, and while her award made me feel really proud, I was also a tad irritated at the need for such a category. While encouragement is great, in business, unlike in sport, gender does not matter. We are all equals. The day when there will be enough Falgunis who would compete alongside successful men for a business person award—that is something worth waiting for!

1) Do you speak up when you see gender-related bias operating at home or work? What holds women back from doing so? What can help?
2) Do you behave like an equal at home and work? Do you practise and encourage equality with your children and colleagues?

The Winning Mindset

It's true that to a large extent, you need the right background, good opportunities and some amount of luck in order to succeed, and yet I can confidently say that many of the women that have been featured here struggled with one or more of these. Some came from such conservative backgrounds that even a college education met with opposition from the family, some have overcome the trauma of domestic abuse, battled infertility or simply resisted society's obsession to get girls married. And through the challenges, they have emerged as fine professionals. It's clear that what saw them through was a winner's mindset, one that made the most of the hand that was dealt to them and one that refused to bow down to challenges. To my mind, a winner is a person who feels happy and fulfilled. They maximize the opportunities that come their way and become the best possible versions of themselves. So here are some of the common traits that I have observed:

1. Winners remain committed to excellence, always. Even if they opt for less-demanding roles, work shorter hours, work from home or need to change tracks, they give it their best and don't compromise on the quality of their work.

2. Quitting work completely never crosses a winner's mind. A winner is certain that her problems, however difficult they may seem at that time, will pass, and for that to happen, she starts looking for solutions. She feels stretched, she gets hassled, she loses sleep, but she never considers quitting totally. And that is because she knows that her journey is a long one and some turbulence on the way is to be expected.

3. Winners learn to let go of what's not important and they are not hard on themselves about what

they are not good at. They see no point in wasting energy trying to please everyone and being better than the others at everything. Instead, they just focus on what they are good at and leave the rest. At the end of the day, it is important to stay happy and fulfilled, not bitter and restless.

4. I find that those who succeed in life give themselves sufficient priority. They work very hard, but don't kill themselves with too many other responsibilities. They invest in domestic help, ask for support from their families and spouses, outsource whatever they can and, most importantly, invest in themselves. They give priority to themselves as they believe in themselves and are proud of the work they do.

5. Winners bring their professional competence to other aspects of their life. Professional women are efficient homemakers as well. They invest in technology and robust support systems.

6. Winners know a good thing when they see one. A supportive employer, an encouraging boss, a workplace that helps you grow are not always easy to come by, so when they find one, they don't easily let go. The same is true of good domestic staff, so they invest in them.

7. More than anything else, a winning mindset is about being fair and positive. Successful women appreciate that men too face their own challenges so they never make their struggles a gender issue. They truly believe that they are Equal, Yet Different.

Acknowledgements

I had never imagined that I would write a book, let alone two. The phenomenal success of the first book gave me the courage to attempt another. Besides, this time, it was a topic that has always been close to my heart. For two years, I worked as a one-woman army; researching, transcribing, writing and rewriting the book. Two long years that left me informed, irritated, occasionally bothered but always enlightened as I was totally consumed by women and their careers.

I would like to thank all the wonderful people who have been candid and generous in sharing their stories and insights. I am grateful to Rama Bijapurkar, Prof. Punam Sahgal, Falguni Nayar, Alpana Parida, Roopa Kudva, Madhabi Puri Buch, Kanchan Jain, S.V. Nathan, K. Ramkumar, Abhijit Bhaduri, Dr Saundarya Rajesh, Promila Ayyangar, Sukanya Kripalu, Sreevidya P., Sunita Venkatraman, Neha Bagaria, Anita Sanghi, Rishi Gour, Dr Anita Patel, Dr Deepa Bhide, Nandini Dias, Anuradha Razdan, Anjali Mohanty,

Deepali Naair, Gauri Chaudhari, Ruchira Chaudhary, Hema Mani, Neha Huddar, Jagriti Kumar, Priya Narendra, Amita Parekh, Arpita, Chitra Ranade, Pallavi Kamath, Dhanashree Shirodkar Joglekar, Doorva Bahuguna, Garima Dikshit, Harkirat Bedi, Maliha Sopariwala, Natasha Ramarathnam, Prerna Bhutani, Prof. Promila Agarwal, Ritu Mohanty, Shubha Lal, Shweta Agarwal, Smita Affinwalla, Sunaina Kapoor, Tejasvi Ravi and Trishna Shah for readily agreeing to make time for me.

While I managed to quote quite a few of the lovely women I had conversations with, I have had to change the names of some as the incidents recounted involved people close to the storyteller. I am grateful that they trusted me enough to share deeply personal anecdotes, with a promise that I would keep their identities safe. While I have tried to capture the unique insight and wisdom that every interview brought, I could only manage to take quotes that were the most telling or were the best articulated thoughts on recurring themes that came up in various discussions. In the process, many of the people whom I interviewed have not got a mention. I want to thank them and say that I value their thoughts just as much.

My sincere gratitude to Sharda Ugra, Pritsikha Anil and Pallavi Kamath. I believe that their early feedback on a preliminary draft eventually led to a better final product. Prem Panicker's sage advice to take a two-week break from writing helped me recharge at a point when I felt overwhelmed by the book as much as by the pandemic.

My family of three men cheered me on and were great sounding boards. I hope they become better husbands, friends and colleagues as a result of what they have learnt in the process.

My friend and well-known author Prakash Iyer introduced me to Penguin Random House and to my editor Radhika Marwah. I remember the day, maybe twenty-five years ago, when Harsha and I had nudged Prakash into picking up the pen. Little did we realize that he would turn out to be so prolific and so successful! Thank you, Prakash.

It has been fun working with Radhika. Having an editor who is also a spontaneous representative of the primary target audience made her inputs doubly valuable. Her comments and suggestions even called out my occasional generational bias and helped me keep the content relevant to today's reader.

Finally, I want to thank Steve Waugh, former captain of the Australian men's cricket team. Quite unknown to him, one of his quotes gave me both the inspiration and the title for this book!

Notes

1) Statistical Profile on Women Labour—2013, Labour Bureau, Government of India; Center for Strategic and International Studies—Wadhwani Chair—2012; Business World Gallup Survey 2006; *Declining Trends in Female Labour Force Participation in India: Evidence from NSSO*—2013.

2) Quoted in *Lean In—Women, Work and the Will to Lead*, Sheryl Sandberg, p. 62.

3) Victoria L. Brescoll, 'Leading with Their Hearts? How Gender Stereotypes of Emotion Lead to Biased Evaluations of Female Leaders', *The Leadership Quarterly*, Department of Organizational Behavior, Yale School of Management, Yale University, P.O. Box 208205, New Haven, CT 06520-8205, USA.

4) 'CS Gender 3000 in 2019—The Changing Face of Companies', CSIR report.

5) https://www.narendramodi.in/vikasyatra/articledetail/transformative-economic-growth/paving-the-path-for-five-trillion-dollar-economy-549917

6) *Economic and Political Weekly*, 3 June 2017, Vol. III, No. 22.